Students Harassing Students

The Emotional and Educational Toll on Kids

Jan Cantrell

ROWMAN & LITTLEFIELD EDUCATION
Lanham • New York • Toronto • Plymouth, UK

Published in the United States of America
by Rowman & Littlefield Education
A Division of Rowman & Littlefield Publishers, Inc.
A wholly owned subsidiary of The Rowman & Littlefield Publishing Group,
Inc.
4501 Forbes Boulevard, Suite 200, Lanham, Maryland 20706
www.rowmaneducation.com

Estover Road
Plymouth PL6 7PY
United Kingdom

British Library Cataloguing in Publication Information Available

Library of Congress Cataloging-in-Publication Data

Cantrell, Jan.
  Students harassing students : the emotional and educational toll on kids /
Jan Cantrell.
     p. cm.
  ISBN-13: 978-1-57886-858-2 (cloth : alk. paper)
  ISBN-10: 1-57886-858-0 (cloth : alk. paper)
  ISBN-13: 978-1-57886-861-2 (pbk. : alk. paper)
  ISBN-10: 1-57886-861-0 (pbk. : alk. paper)
  eISBN-13: 978-1-57886-890-2
  eISBN-10: 1-57886-890-4
  [etc.]
  1. Sexual harassment in education. 2. Students—Abuse of. I. Title.
  LC212.8.C36 2008
  371.5'8—dc22   2008024929

∞™ The paper used in this publication meets the minimum requirements
of American National Standard for Information Sciences—Permanence of
Paper for Printed Library Materials, ANSI/NISO Z39.48-1992.

This book is dedicated to the thousands of students who
have endured humiliation caused by their peers.
It is my fervent hope that this book will help
eliminate peer sexual harassment and make school
a place where kids want to be.

Contents

Acknowledgments

Thanks to Tom Koerner for encouraging me to write this book; to Dr. Brenda Freeman, counselor extraordinaire, for her advice, and especially to Terry, who believes in all my endeavors.

Introduction

Twelve-year-old Alisha can't concentrate on what her science teacher is saying. A male classmate snapped her bra right before class, and Alisha was mortified. She wants to go home.

Roger, an eighth grader, isn't listening to his math teacher because he just read a note from a classmate that warned him that some of the guys were going to take his pants off to check out "his package" when he walks to his next class.

Amy, a junior, is crying because she is tired of being called an "AIDS promoter" and a dyke. She is thinking of dropping out of school.

Fourteen-year-old Carl has been harassed so much since he started middle school that he has started hanging around with the kids who do drugs. At least they don't tease him. Besides, the drugs make him forget that he is called names and physically attacked at least once a month.

Betsy, a second grader, doesn't like it when Todd touches her body and tries to kiss her every day at recess. She gets sick to her stomach often during class. Her teacher thinks she is faking it. Her grades have dropped a lot this year.

What all of these students have in common is that they are being sexually harassed. They are forced to attend school in a hostile environment. It doesn't matter that the youngest victim is seven and the oldest is seventeen. All of them are being harassed, which means they are being hurt emotionally and sometimes physically. The reactions of the school officials vary from a shrug of the shoulders to alarm and outrage. Unfortunately, too many times no one at the school is aware of what is taking place.

When school officials do confront an alleged harasser with his/her actions, many times the student seems surprised. Many of them say they didn't even know they were doing anything wrong. It's no wonder. Kids today are living in a society saturated with sexual messages. Television, movies, and videos contain graphic sexual scenes and obscene language, as do bumper stickers and music. Sports figures and movie stars are convicted of rape and violence, and no one seems to be outraged. Tolerance of indecency and sexual activities among the young seems to be the norm.

Schools are expected to prohibit behavior that seems to be accepted and even applauded in society. When they don't, students are trapped. Unlike an employee who can quit a job, students are under compulsory education laws and must stay in a setting where they are subjected to harassment. Students who have been touched inappropriately or called names such as "slut," "bitch," and "five-cent hole" have reported that they are afraid, ashamed, embarrassed, and powerless. One student summed it up by saying that it "breaks your soul."

The results of large research projects in the past twenty-five years show us that sexual harassment among students in K–12 schools is a huge problem. More than three-fourths of the students surveyed report they have been sexually harassed at school. Aside from the tragic results, which range from feelings of embarrassment and anxiety to severe depression and suicide, there is also the devastating effect that being sexually harassed by other students has on the victims' education: Absenteeism climbs, grades plunge, and dropout rates increase. The learning of the victims is impaired, and their education suffers immeasurably. The effect of that could very well follow them the rest of their lives, thus affecting their chances of success in the adult world.

Nobody ever has the right to make life miserable for another person. Unfortunately, that lesson isn't getting across to students in today's society. Lack of respect for others seems to be rampant, and when parents don't get the message across, students suffer and the schools must step up to the plate to prevent and address student-to-student sexual harassment. It is not nearly enough to just post a nondiscrimination policy on a school website or on the bulletin board in the main office. Schools must be proactive with prevention programs and messages to students that peer sexual harassment will not be tolerated. It is illegal, and it is wrong.

This book is intended for parents and students as well as school personnel. Parents need to be made aware of the scope of the problem, and students need to know that they can get help, and that sexual harassment among students can be decreased. No student should have to go to a school where sexual harassment is tolerated. With parents, students, and school personnel working together, we can prevent peer sexual harassment.

My goal in writing this book is to enlighten teachers, administrators, counselors, and parents concerning the seriousness of the problem of peer sexual harassment issues in schools today. My fervent hope is that those who read this book will be so outraged that they will do more than just shake their heads and say "What a shame." We need people who will take action to fix this problem. The futures and emotional health of young people are at stake here!

I have attempted to present the problem, define it, and offer solutions to it. In addition, I have presented the legal issues and given suggestions to teachers, students, parents, and administrators as to their specific roles. Finally, I have offered a sample policy and sources where the reader can find other policies that have been adopted by school districts.

The reader will notice at a glance that the book contains no cartoons or pictures. That is because there is nothing humorous about the subject matter, and it is too ugly to be illustrated with pictures. Peer sexual harassment is a serious subject and must be taken seriously.

If this book can contribute to one school doing something about peer sexual harassment, or can prevent one student from being hurt, then it will have been worth the time and effort it took to write it.

1

How Big Is the Problem and Why Is It Happening?

SCENARIO

Kindergarten: *"I see London, I see France. I see Susie's underpants!"*

Fourth Grade: *"Hey Susie, if you would quit wearing panties under that skirt, I'd let you sit by me."*

Sixth Grade: *"Hey Susie, Tom and I want to know where you got those big boobs over the summer."*

Eighth Grade: *"Hey Susie, can I put my thing in your thong?"*

Ninth Grade: *"Look Susie. My hand fits right over your boob! Amazing!"*

Tenth Grade: *"I'm sure Jake doesn't mean to keep brushing against you, Susie. The lunch line is just so crowded. Don't worry about the name-calling; your friends know you're not a slut. And I'll try to remember to have the custodian get rid of the graffiti in the bathroom."*

Eleventh Grade: *"Stop it!"*
 "Oh come on, Susie. You know you like it."

Twelfth Grade: *"Where's Susie? Isn't she coming back this year?"*

PREVALENCE

Sexual harassment among students in K–12 schools is no laughing matter. It can escalate, as in the case above, or it can be extremely serious the first time it occurs. It can happen to boys or girls. It can happen to heterosexual or homosexual students. It can happen in a classroom or somewhere else. It can be addressed, or it can be ignored. But whenever or wherever it happens or however it is addressed, it is always detrimental to students and sometimes tragically so.

How common is it?

The prominent and most cited comprehensive report on student sexual harassment was first published by the AAUW in 1993 and revisited in 2001 (AAUW, 2001). The 1993 study surveyed 1,632 students, grades eight to eleven, and the 2001 survey collected responses from 2,064 students. Eighty-three percent of the girls and 60 percent of the boys had been sexually harassed by peers. Thirty-nine percent reported being sexually harassed every day. Another study conducted in 1993 by the Permanent Commission on the Status of Women (1995) reported 78 percent of the 547 students responding had been sexually harassed in school. Other studies reported similar findings. Those statistics should be shocking and unacceptable to educators and parents.

For many students sexual harassment is an ongoing experience. Nobody has the right to sexually harass another person. A more in-depth look reveals the following:

- Eighty-three percent of girls in grades eight to eleven experience some form of sexual harassment during their school lives. Fifty-six percent of boys reported having been sexually harassed.
- More than one in four students experience sexual harassment often.
- Thirty-nine percent of the respondents in one major study reported being harassed daily (Stein et al., 1993).
- Many students report that sexual harassment is the norm in their schools (Fineran, 1998 citing Strauss and Espeland, 1992).
- Six in ten students experience physical sexual harassment at some time during their school life, and one-third of those students experience it more than one time (AAUW, 2001).
- All of the studies indicate that girls are targeted much more than boys. Indications are that over 90 percent of the time male students are the harassers and female students the victims (Stein et al., 1993; Strauss and Espeland, 1992).

- Students as young as kindergarten age are sexually harassed by their peers. Sexual harassment escalates in middle school.
- Two-thirds of the harassment incidents at school occur with other persons present (Koepels, 1999).
- Eleven percent of students report they have been forced to do something sexual other than kissing (Murdock & Kysilko, 1998).
- Studies have shown that peer sexual harassment creates an intrusive educational environment, interferes with learning, and escalates when ignored. Students have reported that they feel threatened, depressed, even suicidal (Stone & Couch 2004).
- Large numbers of girls (33 percent) report not wanting to go to school, not wanting to talk in class, and finding it hard to pay attention (Koepels, 1999).
- Students of both genders who are sexually harassed have a higher rate of absenteeism from school, lower concentration in class, and less participation in class. They also report sleep disturbances, loss of appetite, feelings of anger, feelings of being threatened and being upset, as well as low self-esteem and lack of confidence (Fineran, 1998).

These statistics must not be ignored. A sad observation is that in 1993 only 26 percent of the students surveyed reported that their schools had a sexual harassment policy, but 69 percent of the students reported such a policy was in place in their schools in 2001 (AAUW, 2001). Yet the incidence of sexual harassment *increased* during that time period.

That suggests that the policies do not deter sexual harassment incidents. However, school personnel are much more likely to intervene in sexual harassment incidents if there is a school policy that is enforced (Stein et al., 1993). That last statement may be a poor reflection on school personnel. Teachers and others should not have to be threatened by a policy to do the right thing and prevent peer sexual harassment in our schools. One can only hope that they are more apt to intervene when policy is enforced because they are better informed than those in schools without policy enforcement.

In medium to large high schools not a day goes by when a student does not sexually harass another student. But harassment is not limited to those schools. Students in rural areas and those enrolled in private school report sexual harassment incidents as well (Stone & Couch, 2004). Peer student harassment is a pervasive problem. It is not limited to schools in the United States (DeSouza, & Ribeiro, 2005; Witkowska, E., 2005).

Numerous incidents of sexual harassment have been reported in elementary schools, and several of those incidents have resulted in lawsuits against the school. Middle schools and high schools also have their share of sexual harassment incidents, and in fact, middle school has been suggested to be the location of the highest percentage of peer sexual harassment incidents. Nor is peer sexual harassment limited to one race or culture; however, because of cultural differences, the perceptions of what constitutes sexual harassment may differ, as well as the responses by the students being harassed.

WHY DO STUDENTS HARASS OTHER STUDENTS?

Even with all of the attention that peer sexual harassment in the school setting has received, it does not seem to be decreasing. Too many people seem to view the incidents as normal school occurrences and normal adolescent social-sexual behavior. In some cultures sexual harassment is tolerated because male power structures are embedded within the patriarchal nature of the culture.

Most researchers agree that the intent of sexual harassment is to demean, embarrass, humiliate, or control another person on the basis of that person's gender or sexual orientation. But the question that needs to be answered is: Why do the harassers *want* to demean or humiliate and control another person? Why do they want to embarrass or humiliate other students? That leads to the victims believing that they are indeed weaker, of lesser value, and in many cases helpless.

Like any behavior problem at school, simply reacting to the situation is not enough. We must discover the cause for the behavior and attack the problem using preventive measures. Look at some of the reasons students harass their peers:

Reasons for Sexual Harassment among Peers

Reason #1

The student is unaware the action was sexual harassment or unwelcome. Many times students who are accused of sexually harassing a peer are not aware that their actions were considered sexual harassment.

"I was just kidding."

"Everybody says (does) that."

"She (he) thought it was funny. What's wrong with making someone laugh?"

Twenty-four percent of students who harass their peers report that they thought the person liked it (AAUW, 2001). In other words, they did not know the action was unwelcome. Twenty-six percent said they "wanted a date with the person" (p. 41.)

As educators it is our responsibility both legally and morally to define sexual harassment for them. Sexual harassment will be defined in chapter 2.

Reason #2

The student is trying to look "cool" in front of her/his peers. There are numerous incidents of sexual harassment reported annually within elementary schools, but a student's first experience with sexual harassment is most likely to occur in middle school/junior high (AAUW, 2001). Because initial sexual harassment incidents are the most prevalent during the middle school ages, educators often blame the incidents on "raging hormones" and too often ignore the harm they can cause.

As any of us who have taught at the middle school/junior high level can attest, when students leave the smaller and safer environment of elementary school they are often intimidated. They are thrust into a large setting with students they do not know from several other elementary schools. For some students, middle school is the first time they have had to change rooms several times a day and the first time they have no friends in their classes or their lunch period. Added to that are their physical changes and other characteristics of adolescence. Even the most confident young boy or girl can be intimidated in such a setting.

Self-esteem has been shown to decline from sixth through eighth grade. Boys may want to appear powerful and "in charge" even though they may not feel that way. If a seventh-grade boy is harassed by an older student or sees incidents of harassment that other students think are funny, he may in turn harass a student to gain power, to "fit in with the guys," or to prevent his peers from harassing him if he appears weak in their eyes.

The AAUW report (2001) found that 24 percent of harassers of either gender did so because "My friend 'pushed' me into doing it"

(p. 41). It is doubtful that tearing down others ever results in feelings of true self-worth, and ironically, while the harasser is trying to build up his own image, his/her actions are chipping away at the self-esteem of the victims—sometimes to the point of totally destroying that person's self-worth. A student interviewed by Nan Stein and quoted in a government document put it this way: "First of all, let me say that being sexually harassed since 5th grade has gone beyond the damage of affecting the way I feel. . . . Now . . . I have no pride, no self-confidence, and still no way out of the misery I am put through in my school" (OCR, n.d.b.).

That is not to say, however, that all students who sexually harass others have poor self-esteem. Sexual harassment is a form of bullying, and bullies often have very positive self-esteem. McGrath (2007) suggests four possible psychological reasons for bullying: (1) a strong need for power, (2) family conditions, (3) benefits and rewards (perhaps sexual favors), and (4) prestige. The first and last suggestions, need for power and prestige, seem to fit into the category of a student with low self-esteem, but not always. Some students simply crave attention, are intolerant of differences, have a strong need to dominate others, have a sense of entitlement, or want to use others (McGrath, 2007 citing Olweus and Coloroso).

Reason #3

The actions are accepted as normal. "It's just a part of school life/a lot of people do it" was the response from 43 percent of the boys and 34 percent of the girls who responded to the AAUW survey (2001). By the time students enter high school they have often been in an environment where sexual harassment is tolerated and even approved by their peers for three years. In many instances they have observed that little or no action is taken against the harasser(s), and so it continues to be a part of the school culture, dismissed as "normal for that age."

A majority of the students who claimed to have been sexually harassed had, in turn, sexually harassed another student (AAUW, 2001). Certainly not all students who have been sexually harassed by a peer will sexually harass another student, but this does suggest that many students who feel degraded react by degrading someone else, continuing the cycle.

High school students most often report harassment to their friends instead of to an adult, and nothing is done about the incidents. Victims of sexual harassment do indeed feel humiliated and powerless to prevent the harassment, and so the behavior continues.

Reason #4

Students harass peers to gain power and status. Sexual harassment is about power and status, and it is typically perpetrated by someone having power over someone with lower status or power (Anderson, 2006). In the case of peer harassment in schools, the harassers have no right of power over other students. In other words, unlike employer/employee relationships, students are equally powerful. Boys may think they are more powerful than girls; aggressive girls may perceive themselves as more powerful than less popular girls or boys; athletes may consider themselves as deserving more power in the culture of school; school leaders may consider themselves in positions of power over less popular students. But the reality is that none of those students has the right to exert dominance over another student.

Of course the athletes, school leaders, and members of the popular crowd are certainly not the only students guilty of sexual harassment, and most of them would never consider harassing another student. These school leaders are the very ones who should be modeling non-harassing behavior.

Reason #5

Students continue to sexually harass peers because nothing is done about it. When school personnel turn a blind eye to what is going on in their schools, nothing will change to stop the behaviors. Consider these cases:

1. An elementary student in Minnesota was continually harassed about her body parts and was told to have oral sex with her father. Nothing was done, as the district officials determined that with children that young the actions were simply "misbehavior."
2. The parents of a senior high school student in Minnesota asked sixteen times for school officials to remove the obscene remarks about their daughter from the bathroom walls. The graffiti remained in place for eighteen months. The principal's attitude was "where there is smoke there is fire" (Yaffee, 1995 quoting Stein & Sjostrom, 1994).

3. A kindergarten student in Texas assaulted five-year-old Jane Doe, shoving his hand in her vagina, resulting in bleeding, pain, and hematuria. The principal took no action, wrote no report, and did not contact either set of parents. Jane became depressed, could not sleep, and developed suicidal tendencies. The district ignored Jane's mother's request that they guarantee her safety. When Jane's mother took her out of school, the school threatened truancy proceedings (*Jane Doe v. Dallas Independent School District*, 2002).

4. Three elementary girls from Sarasota reported that a male classmate continually subjected them to vulgar remarks and gestures, including pointing to his genital area and telling them to "suck it," rubbing against them, and telling them to have sex with him. The girls reported the incidents to a teacher, but nothing was done (*Hawkins v. Sarasota County School Board*, 2003).

Those are just a few examples. In those cases the victims reported responses including extreme distress, pain, crying, unwillingness to go to school, thoughts of suicide, and stress that lasted for years following the incidents.

There are many reasons for peer sexual harassment in our schools. Knowing how to prevent peer sexual harassment is necessary. We need to be shocked enough to do something about it, as it is not only devastating for students, but it carries over into society as those students become adults.

Identifying some of the reasons why students sexually harass their peers will give those who work with students, including teachers, counselors, social workers, and parents, some idea of the root of the problem.

CASE STUDY

Background

Hilltop Elementary has a student population of 546 students, grades K–5. The school has a good reputation, and parents often request that their children be allowed to transfer into Hilltop from other schools in the district. Two months ago three of the fifth-grade teachers attended a national education conference on school climate. They have discussed what they learned informally with some of their colleagues but have not been approached to present any in-service information.

Participants

Becca Roberts, Cynthia Alvarez, and Lucy Crandall, fifth-grade teachers

Danny Montego, principal

Theresa Upton, assistant principal in charge of student discipline

Mark Willard, a sixth-grade student

Darla Lund, and Tara Bock, fifth-grade girls

Incident

Tara approached her teacher's desk at lunchtime.

Tara Bock: Ms. Crandall, Mark just called Darla a slut. She is really mad, too. He keeps saying really bad things to her.

Lucy Crandall: Like what, Tara? What does he say?

Tara: Oh you know. He uses words that we're not supposed to say like "whore" and "bitch." If I ever said those words my parents would ground me for life!

Lucy: OK Tara, I'll talk to Mark.

Tara: Please don't tell him who told you, OK?

Lucy: Don't worry about it, Tara. Just run on to lunch.

A few minutes later Lucy Crandall put her tray on the table in the teachers' lounge and sat down by her colleagues, Becca and Cynthia.

Lucy: Mark Willard is at it again. This time Tara said he called Darla Land disgusting names. I've already warned him about that twice. I even told the eighth-grade counselor. I think I'll send him to see Ms. Upton.

Becca: Just for calling a girl names? C'mon, Lucy. The kids call each other names like "bitch" all the time. They think nothing of it. And you know what Mr. Montego said about handling discipline ourselves. He is adamant about that. I'm telling you—the kids don't really mind. Tara Bock is just overprotected. Darla probably didn't mind as much as Tara did.

Lucy: Maybe not, but I do! It might be the in way to talk now, but I still think it's disgusting and degrading. How would you like to be called a slut?

Becca: Remember, Luce, I've only been out of high school three years. That was just normal talk in our school. What do you think, Cynthia?

Cynthia: Honestly, before last week's conference I guess I would have just ignored it, but I attended a session on sexual harassment issues and the speaker said that name-calling falls under that category. He also said that in a situation like that the other kids who hear the name-calling may be being harassed too.

Becca: Give me a break. If every girl who was called a name claimed she was sexually harassed we'd be bogged down in claims!

Cynthia: So? If that's what it takes to clean up the halls, maybe we need to tell the students to complain about being called names.

Lucy: In the meantime, I guess I'll just talk to Mark. One more time! After that I'm calling his parents.

Becca: You better hope your talk works, Luce. I've heard his dad is really mean.

Cynthia: Oh so now we're supposed to be afraid of a parent?

Becca: No. I'm just saying sometimes it's better to let sleeping dogs lie.

Lucy: There's the bell. Thanks for listening, you two. Although I can't really say you helped much.

Becca: Want some advice, Luce? Don't make a big deal of it. I heard one of the eighth-grade girls got her bra taken off of her in the boys' bathroom earlier this year and all Ms. Upton did was write up the incident and put it in the boys' files.

Two weeks later in the principal's office:

Mr. Montego: I asked you in here, Ms. Crandall, because we seem to have a problem. Not one, but two parents have called me this morning very upset. It seems as though one of the sixth-grade boys has been bothering their daughters. Actually, they said "harassing." Whatever. Parents of girls are paranoid sometimes. Anyway, those things happen, and we'll deal with it. But what concerns me is that both parents said their daughters said that you knew about the incidents and did nothing about them. Yesterday the so-called "harasser" went a little too far and got caught writing Darla Lund's name on the board in a classroom before lunch with the words "Slut Butt" in parenthesis. Several students who were in the room saw it and got quite a kick out of it. The worst part is, though, that evidently at least one of the girls had told you twice before that Mark had said some unkind things to girls. Personally I think that is just what thirteen-year-old boys do, but maybe it is getting out of hand. Mrs. Lund suggested that if I didn't call Mark's parents, she would. She was really steamed that we hadn't handled this before. So why didn't you do anything about the complaints?

Discussion questions:

1. Did these incidents constitute sexual harassment? If so, who was being harassed?
2. What criteria should you use to determine the answer?
3. What should the teacher(s) have done?
4. Who was at fault in this situation?
5. How realistic is the case study?
6. What might have prevented this situation from occurring more than once?

The following chapters will provide some answers to those questions.

2

What Is Sexual Harassment?

FIRST SCENARIO

Olivia waited in the girls' restroom as long as she could without being tardy before hurrying to her third-hour class. She slid into her seat just as the tardy bell rang. Mr. Rotz, her English teacher, raised his eyebrow.

"Cutting it a little close, aren't you, Olivia? You barely make it every day. What's the problem? Can't leave your friends even for fifty minutes?"

Olivia heard a snicker behind her, and she knew without turning around who it was. Robert. He was a friend of Ron and Will, and he knew exactly why Olivia came to class late.

For the past six weeks Ron Kurtz and Will Johnson had been taunting and teasing Olivia. They called her "Ollie Oyl" and asked her daily how anyone could have "such a big behind" and nothing at all to balance it out on top.

"Oh golly, Skinny Ollie,
All we can find is your behind!"

First Olivia tried to ignore the boys. She certainly couldn't tell a teacher or counselor—Ron and Will were big football players. Everybody thought they were so cool. Even Olivia's two friends, Kathryn and Beth, thought the boys were cool. She couldn't risk losing her friends' approval. When Olivia had mentioned that she was going to report the boys to the sophomore counselor, Beth had strongly advised her that she would be ruining her social life forever.

13

Chapter 2

Big deal. As far as Olivia could tell, she had no social life. The boys waited for her every day before third hour to recite their little poem. Whatever kids were in the hall laughed and laughed. Lately Olivia had thought about cutting her morning classes every day. Sure, she would eventually get caught, but surely it wouldn't be any worse than this. Besides, her grades in second hour had gone from A's to C's and D's. She spent the last half of that class worrying about how to avoid the boys on her way to English. Lately she had been locking herself in a bathroom stall until just before the tardy bell rang.

Is Olivia being sexually harassed, or is this just "boys being boys"? What if she were seven instead of fifteen? What if *girls* were calling her names instead of boys? What if it didn't bother her? Would it be sexual harassment then? What is sexual harassment anyway?

Although sexual harassment has undoubtedly been around for as long as recorded history, it was brought to national attention in the United States during the U.S. Supreme Court confirmation hearings of Clarence Thomas when Anita Hill testified. Since that time the term *sexual harassment* has become commonplace, and sexual harassment issues have been litigated at all levels of the court system. Most of the litigation has involved sexual harassment issues concerning employees being harassed by employers or other subordinates such as students being sexually harassed by teachers or other adults in the school setting. It is becoming more and more common, however, to hear about students being harassed by other students—peer/peer sexual harassment.

Fineran and Bennett (2000) point out that much of society typically views sexual harassment experiences of middle and high school students as part of normal adolescent development, causing it to be overlooked for the hurtful behavior it is. "The failure to acknowledge sexual harassment in schools and the traditional tendency to dismiss student conduct simply as 'kids being kids' is no longer acceptable" (Dragen, 2006, p. 1). Daily in our schools, students from ages five to eighteen are being hurt emotionally and sometimes physically. The results are never good. In some cases they are tragic. The violence at Columbine, at Virginia Tech, and in numerous other school settings has reinforced what we already knew—students who don't feel accepted by their peers, who are being bullied, or who feel like they are being looked down upon are too often time bombs for disaster. Whether it is actual or just perceived, sexual harassment is a form of bullying, and it has reached epidemic proportions in our schools.

Before school officials can stop peer/peer sexual harassment from occurring, they must know what it is. The first step in eliminating the problem is to define it. Only when administrators, teachers, and other school personnel are aware of what constitutes sexual harassment will they be able to put a stop to it in their schools.

DEFINITION

A simple definition of sexual harassment is "any unwelcome behavior of a sexual nature that interferes with the life of the target(s); it is un-solicited and nonreciprocal" (Shoop & Edwards, 1994, p. 17). Other definitions include the definition provided by the Equal Employment Opportunity Commission (EEOC), which states that like other forms of sexual assault,

> sexual harassment includes a wide range of behaviors including unwel-come sexual advances, requests for sexual favors, and other verbal or physical conduct of a sexual nature, when submission to or rejection of this conduct explicitly or implicitly affects an individual's employment, unreasonably interferes with an individual's work performance or cre-ates an intimidating, hostile or offensive work environment. (U.S. Equal Employment Opportunity Commission, 1990, p. 1)

That definition is easy to understand and applies to employers and employees, but Olivia from the scenario above is not in a work setting. She is a student in a public school. So is it sexual harassment? Further definitions are necessary to determine what constitutes sexual harass-ment among students in school settings.

Legally, sexual harassment is considered a form of sex discrimina-tion. It is specifically prohibited by federal laws and several state laws. Title VII of the Civil Rights Act of 1964 has been extended by some courts to include peer harassment in school, and Title IX of the Edu-cation Amendments of 1972 has been used to show liability of the school systems (Schwartz, 2000).

Unwelcomeness

Definitions of sexual harassment always include the word *unwelcome* to describe behavior or actions. According to the government, conduct is unwelcome if the student does not request or invite it and views the action as offensive or undesirable. It is not the same as flirting. Flirting results in positive self-esteem and it is legal and desirable. Whereas flirting makes the receiver feel good, sexual harassment makes the receiver feel powerless and demeaned. It results in negative self-esteem and is illegal.

It is not easy for an observer to be sure that the behavior is unwelcome. A student who is being harassed may consent or at least not appear to be bothered by the remarks or actions, but that reaction may be a defensive reaction to keep peers from further harassment or bullying, or simply a way to gain popularity.

Unwelcomeness means just that. It is in the mind of the victim. That means that a student may be accused of sexual harassment even if he/she didn't intend to harm the person. Intent has nothing to do with it. If the actions or words are disrespectful and not something that the person would say or do if a parent or teacher were around, there is a strong possibility that the action is unwelcome and constitutes sexual harassment.

According to the OCR, conduct is unwelcome if "the student did not request or invite it and regarded the conduct as undesirable or offensive." (OCR, 2001, p. 53). The OCR guidance goes on to stress that just because a student does not complain, it does not mean that she/he welcomed the action. The student may not complain out of fear.

For evidence of whether or not an action was unwelcome, investigators may look at the credibility of the harassed student and the harasser, look to see if the alleged harasser has harassed other students, look at the behavior of the harassed student immediately following the incident, and check to see if there were witnesses to the incident who could state the action was unwelcome. Of course the best indicator of whether or not the action was unwelcome is what the alleged victim says.

Laws regarding sexual harassment do not require that schools forbid flirting, dating, or giving compliments or actions that are welcomed by the receiver. They do prohibit behavior that is exploitative or demeaning, based on an imbalance of power. It has been suggested that students could be told "It is ok to date, but not to intimidate" (Murdock & Kysilko, 1998, p. 7).

Unwelcomeness is a matter of the victim's perspective. The behavior might be unwelcome, but the victim may be hesitant or scared to let the violator know it is unwelcome. What is unwelcome to one student may be acceptable to another. Students should be taught that if there is a question as to whether the action would be offensive or not, they should refrain from the comment or action. Murdock (1998) suggests the following questions students should ask themselves to determine unwelcomeness:

Have I been told my actions are unwelcome or inappropriate?
Would I say or do this if my parent, girlfriend, boyfriend, or teacher were present?
Would I want someone to say or do this to my sister or brother or boyfriend or girlfriend?
Would I want my actions to be on the evening news?
Is the person to whom I'm saying this in an equal position of power as I am?
Do my actions show respect for the other person?

The age of the student must be taken into consideration and the language of the questions adjusted accordingly.

The Office of Civil Rights (OCR) lists the following examples of conduct that could be considered sexual harassment if unwelcome:

- Direct or indirect threats or bribes for unwanted sexual activity
- Sexual innuendos and comments
- Intrusive sexually explicit questions
- Sexually suggestive sounds or gestures such as sucking noises, winks, or pelvic thrusts
- Repeatedly asking a person out for dates or to have sex
- Touching, patting, pinching, stroking, squeezing, tickling, or brushing against a person
- A neck/shoulder massage
- Rating a person's sexual attractiveness
- Ogling, leering, or staring at a woman's breasts or a man's derriere
- Spreading rumors about a person's sexuality
- Graffiti about a person's sexuality
- Name-calling such as "bitch," "whore," or "slut"
- Sexual ridicule
- Frequent jokes about sex
- Letters, notes, telephone calls, or material of a sexual nature
- Pervasive displays of picture calendars, cartoons, or other materials with sexually explicit graphic content

- Stalking a person
- Attempted or actual sexual assault (OCR, 2001).

Other definitions include:

- Sexual graffiti or messages on bathroom walls
- Called gay or lesbian using derogatory terms like "fag" or "lezzie"
- Spied on while dressing or showering at school
- Flashed or mooned
- Clothing pulled down or off
- Spiking (pulling down someone's pants) or "snuggies" (when underwear is pulled up at the waist) (AAUW, 1993; Permanent Commission on the Status of Women [PSCW], 1995; Strauss & Espeland, 1992, as cited in AAUW, 1993).

So the questions are:

1. Does the behavior by the boys toward Olivia fall under any of the definitions from the above lists?
2. Does it make a difference that the boys never mentioned the word "sex" in their taunting?
3. If Olivia tells her teacher about the name-calling, should the teacher treat it as sexual harassment, or just rudeness?

As you ponder those questions, let's take a look at one of Olivia's peers.

SECOND SCENARIO

Lisa grabbed her jacket, locked her car door, and dashed across the parking lot. It had taken her so long to find a parking place that she had almost lost sight of Trevor and Kent and Marrianne. They were just entering the commons area when she caught up to them. Kent was talking to Marrianne.

"Hey, Sexy," Kent said, winking. "What's that hot little bod of yours going to be doing around 2:45 this afternoon?"

Marrianne laughed. "I dunno. What would you like this 'hot little bod' to be doing?"

"I'll tell you what, Sweet Thing. Meet me in the annex of the boys' gym and I'll show you." Kent nudged Trevor, who laughed. "In fact I'll make the

temp of that bod break the heat barrier. Wanna come too, Lisa? We could make it a threesome."

Trevor punched him in the shoulder. "Watch it, my man. If Lisa ever does realize that virginity is not all it's cracked up to be, I get first shot."

Lisa ducked her head, and Kent laughed. "Come on, Leese. Give us what we want. You don't want to be the only one not invited to prom, do you?"

Lisa looked up quickly. Marrianne put her arm around Lisa's shoulder. "Hey guys, leave her alone. If she doesn't get to go to prom, we'll tell her about it. There's something sweet about 'saving yourself' for marriage," Marrianne said, making quotation marks with her fingers.

Lisa cringed. She had thought Marrianne understood, but evidently she didn't. Lately every conversation the four of them had led to talking about Lisa's virginity. Yesterday Marrianne told her that she had heard some of the other junior boys discussing it. She wondered if the famous "Hall of Fame and Shame" in the guys' restroom had her name on it.

All of a sudden Lisa wasn't so eager to get to school. Maybe it would have been better if she hadn't found a parking spot at all. Who cared about school anyway? Lisa thought about it all during history class. Before second period started she went to the office and called her mom to tell her she had a splitting headache and was coming home.

The questions in Lisa's dilemma are somewhat different.

1. Were the comments made by her friends sexual harassment?
2. Does it make a difference that she willingly ran around with Marrianne, Kent, and Trevor?
3. Does it make a difference that this was not the first embarrassing conversation she had been in with the other three?
4. If the "Hall of Fame and Shame" does exist on the wall in the boys' bathroom, is that a form of sexual harassment?

MORE TO THE DEFINITION

The Office for Civil Rights designates two types of conduct that constitute sexual harassment. The first, quid pro quo, applies when an employer or someone in a superior position is involved and conditions a person's participation in an activity or bases a decision on the subordinate's submission to unwelcome sexual advances, requests for sexual favors, or other conduct of a sexual nature (OCR, 2001). In a

school setting an example of this type of harassment would be a
teacher or other school official telling a student his/her grade or place
on a team would be affected by the student's willingness to perform
certain acts.

The other type of harassment is the one under which peer/peer sexual harassment falls: hostile environment. Hostile environment sexual harassment as defined by the OCR:

> can include unwelcome sexual advances, requests for sexual favors, and
> other verbal, nonverbal, or physical conduct of a sexual nature by an em-
> ployee, *by another student* [emphasis added], or by a third party that is
> sufficiently severe, persistent, or pervasive to limit a student's ability to
> participate in or benefit from an educational program, or activity, or to
> create a hostile or abusive educational environment. (OCR, 2001)

When ascertaining whether or not an incident constitutes sexual harassment, then, school officials must look at these three criteria: (1)
severity, (2) persistence, and (3) pervasiveness of the incident. However, all three criteria do not need to be present. For example, the harassment does not have to occur more than once (be persistent) to
constitute harassment if it is severe and/or pervasive. Likewise, name-
calling, for example, may not be considered severe or pervasive, but if
it constantly occurs, it could constitute sexual harassment under hostile environment criteria.

To be considered a hostile environment, however, it must be shown
that the action is limiting the student's ability to participate or benefit from an educational program or activity or is actually putting the
student in a hostile environment.

Before we evaluate Lisa's situation, let's take a look at two more students.

THIRD SCENARIO

*James walked up to Mrs. Lawson's desk and turned in his homework. Wait-
ing for the other kids to finish, he glanced over at the Fearless Four—Dale
High's outstanding linebackers. He knew they were taunting Krysta again.
They did it every day in this class; passing her notes with obscene suggestions
on them. After the first two notes, Krysta had ignored them and simply
thrown the notes in the garbage can. More than once, though, James had seen*

her crying after class. He liked Krysta. She was smart, quiet, and kind. After class James walked up to Mark, one of the Fearless Four.

"Hey man, why don't you leave her alone? She never did anything to you." Then he walked away.

Three hours later Mark sought him out. "Hey fag, why do you care what happens to the little twit? You want a piece of her?" With that he pulled down his pants and mooned James. James just shook his head in disgust and walked away.

Was Krysta being sexually harassed? Was James? According to the lists of examples provided by the OCR and by the American Association of University Women, both incidents would be considered sexual harassment. Olivia from the first scenario was taunted about her figure, and Lisa, in the second scenario, was the object of sexual innuendos and comments. Likewise, Krysta, from the third scenario, was sent obscene notes, and James, her defender, was mooned. All of the actions were offensive and fall under one or more of the examples. In each case school officials should act.

But how serious were the offenses? Let's take another look at the guidelines from the Office for Civil Rights. Were any of the actions sufficiently *severe, persistent,* or *pervasive* enough to limit the student's ability to participate in or benefit from an educational program? It is only necessary for the behavior to fit into one of the categories to be considered harassment. Using the following working definitions, let's look at each of the terms separately and apply them to the scenarios.

Severe = "inflicting pain or distress" (Merriam-Webster, 2004). To be severe, an action does not have to happen more than once. Physical assault would be considered severe, as would even the threat of bodily harm.

For example, in 1999 a Tenth Circuit Court found that a male student's actions were indeed severe when he repeatedly took a developmentally and physically disabled female student to a secluded area and sexually assaulted her (*Murrell v. School District No. 1*, 1999) Likewise a Sixth Circuit Court found the action severe when a sixth-grade girl was asked to describe oral sex, called names, and had her hair grabbed by a boy while being held down by two other boys, was shoved into a wall, and had her homework destroyed.(*Vance v. Spencer County Public School District*, 2000).

It is not difficult to label those two cases severe by anyone's standards. However, incidents much less serious would also be considered severe if those actions inflicted pain or distress. Students who are called names are indeed being put in a painful situation and are distressed by the actions. Listening to obscene talk could cause distress. Name-calling is obviously not as severe as a physical attack would be, so it is necessary to examine the other two criteria before making a decision.

Persistent = lasting a long time; continuing, unrelenting, or incessant (Merriam-Webster, 2004). Was the student repeatedly taunted and called names?

3. *Pervasive* = to become diffused throughout; present everywhere (Merriam-Webster, 2004). To be considered pervasive the action would be most places the student goes within the school environment. The very idea of a student being surrounded with sexual harassment everywhere at school is odious.

Using those three terms and looking at table 2.1, determine whether or not the students in the scenarios were being sexually harassed.

All of the incidents caused distress, so while some may seem more severe than others, all were severe to some degree. Charting the incidents gives us an idea of how difficult it would be to determine if an action falls under sexual harassment. It also reinforces the necessity of using clearly defined terms and not just some person's opinion.

Defining sexual harassment seems to be subjective. But two things must be noted here: (1) the OCR and later the Supreme Court did not say *all* of the questions had to be answered affirmatively and (2) the guidelines do say that for a school to be held liable the student's participation or benefit from the educational program or activity must have been limited or there must have been a hostile environment.

In the three cases above, all four of the students were being sexually harassed. In at least the first two cases (Olivia and Lisa), the student's ability to participate in or benefit from an educational program was af-

Table 2.1.

Student Pervasive?	Incident	Severe?	Persistent?
Olivia	Taunted about her figure		
Lisa	Friends pressed her to lose her virginity		
Krysta	Sent obscene notes		
James	Called "fag" and mooned		

fected. Neither girl was dropping out of school, but both of them were concentrating on the incidents instead of participating in the educational program. In the first case, Olivia's grades had already suffered.

Krysta, the student who was being sent the obscene notes, seemed to be ignoring them, but the action was persistent, and she could not escape it, as it was in her classroom. The action against James (mooning by a classmate) occurred only once and was not pervasive; however it could be considered severe. Take another look at the chart, and then reexamine each criterion. Remember that "severe" can mean only inflicting distress. Whether or not the incident caused distress can be determined by the reaction of the student being harassed. Olivia's grades suffered; Lisa left school; Krysta cried; James shrugged off the mooning. The analysis of each incident using just the three criteria would look like table 2.2.

We have no evidence that any school official had knowledge of the actions, so at this point the discussion is not about the school's liability. What it is always about, however, is that students were being harmed.

There are many reasons a student will not report incidents like those above to school personnel. One of them is that the student is not aware that the incident constituted sexual harassment. Students, as well as school personnel, must be aware of the definitions, and the easiest explanation is to give them a list of examples like the ones supplied by the OCR and the AAUW that are listed above. The students need to be told that sexual harassment is an unwelcome action and is different from flirting.

We will look at one more incident.

Table 2.2.

Student	Incident	Severe?	Persistent?	Pervasive?
Olivia	Taunted about her figure	Yes (caused distress)	Yes	Yes
Lisa	Friends pressed her to lose her virginity	Yes (caused distress)	Yes	No
Krysta	Sent obscene notes	(caused distress)	Yes	No
James	Called "fag" and mooned	Yes	No	No

FOURTH SCENARIO

Jason and Kevin had been friends since kindergarten. They were an unlikely pair. Jason was the school's star basketball player and had already been offered a scholarship to a Big Twelve school. Lots of girls wanted to date him. Kevin had never had a girlfriend and at five feet, seven inches, 115 pounds, did not play any sport. He had gone out for baseball once and then tried out for the wrestling team, but seemed to have no talent for either one and had soon dropped out of each sport. Nevertheless, Jason and Kevin remained best friends

It had started in ninth grade, the year the boys moved to the new high school. One of the "popular" girls had asked Jason why he, who was so obviously a ten on every physique scale from one to ten, would hang around with Kevin, who was about a two on any "good bod" scale. Then the chant began:

"Hey Ten,
Man of Men,
Why would you
Stick with a gay Number Two?"

And so it was at least once or twice every semester when the two friends were walking down the hall or eating lunch. At first Jason had protested, but Kevin assured him he thought it was funny. He didn't, of course. Once when he said offhand to the chemistry teacher that he wished the girls wouldn't say that, the teacher had replied, "They're just kidding. Show them that you can take it like a man, Kev."

Sexual harassment? Look at the criteria by asking and answering the following questions:

1. Is the action on the list of examples supplied by the OCR? Yes. It falls under both sexual innuendos and comment, and also under rating a person's attractiveness (OCR, 1991).
2. Was the action unwelcome? Yes, it was, but to our knowledge Kevin did not ever tell the students to stop rating him in that way.
3. Was the action severe? Perhaps, as it did cause distress.
4. Was it persistent? Yes. Occurring once or twice a semester doesn't seem like very often, but it was persistent.
5. Was it pervasive? Probably. Actions occurring in school hallways often fall under this category.

Two more questions:

1. Is this the type of harassment that many adults consider "kids being kids," or "just a normal part of being in high school"? Absolutely.
2. Was this affecting the student's education? Although we don't have enough evidence to make that determination, there is little doubt that constant disparaging comments have an emotional effect on anybody. It certainly wasn't making Kevin feel good about himself.

Before it can be addressed and eliminated, peer/peer sexual harassment must be defined. The Office for Civil Rights has provided an excellent list of examples of sexual harassment as well as a definition of harassment leading to a hostile environment. Title IX has provided three terms administrators must use to determine the seriousness of the allegations. One more definition that would seem to be easier for students to understand is this one taken from the Ontario Secondary School Teachers' Federation (1994).

> Sexual harassment is "unwanted and unwelcome sexual behavior which interferes with your life . . . is not behaviors that you like or want (for example, wanted kissing, touching or flirting). It includes putdowns or negative comments about your gender. It is deliberate and/or repeated sexual or sex-based behavior that is not welcome, not asked for, and not returned. (p. 2)

The difficulty lies in getting students to come forward when they are being sexually harassed and in the responses of the school personnel. Both of those issues will be addressed in later chapters.

CASE STUDY

Directions: Using only the criteria of severe, persistent, and/or pervasive, decide whether the following situation would be considered sexual harassment.

Background

Centennial High School has a student population of 2,600 and is located in a small city on the West Coast. One of the electives offered at the school is a class called Publishing and Producing: Graphic Arts and Beyond. That class is responsible for producing the school yearbook. The class meets every day, and as deadlines approach the teacher also requires students to meet after school for two hours twice a week. This year's staff is excited because for the first time the school yearbook will be completely electronic, and students will be able to download it onto their MySpace account.

Participants

Todd is a senior and editor of the yearbook. He is also editor of the school paper and in that role he writes a monthly column for the paper. He is known as a "funny guy" who often makes fun of "jocks and other big shots on campus." He is very intelligent and takes every AP class he can schedule.

Mr. Brock is a second-year teacher. In addition to teaching the yearbook class he teaches four sections of junior language arts. He is well liked by the students.

Ryan is another senior boy in the class.

Carrie is a senior girl who dates Todd occasionally.

Melanie and Shonda are the only two sophomores in the class.

Other students enrolled in the yearbook class are three senior boys and three junior boys. There are also three senior girls and five junior girls.

Incident

It is Thursday afternoon at 3:45. School has been out for thirty minutes, and the halls are clear. The sixteen members of the yearbook staff are meeting in the yearbook room to select the final pictures to be included in the yearbook. Mr. Brock is leaned back in his chair grading papers on his laptop.

Todd: OK, Dudes and Dudettes, to get you all to wake up I'm gonna tell a really good joke.

A couple of the girls roll their eyes. They've heard Todd's idea of "a really good joke" before.

Two or Three Students: Yeah! You go, man! Make it good.

Ryan: Yeah. We like it when it's goooooodd.

Todd: Well, you see, there was this really naive couple. They were probably slow or something. Anyway, this was in the days before birth control pills, and they just kept having children. Finally they went to a doctor and he gave them some condoms. A few months later they were back in the doctor's office and sure enough, the chick was pregnant again. The doctor said, "Didn't you follow the directions on the package?"

"Yes, we did," the woman said. "But it said, 'Place on organ,' and all we had was a piano."

The class groaned.

Ryan: That was lame. I will say, though, it wasn't "limp."

More groans and laughter.

Carrrie (laughing): Todd Beckam, that was bad. What if your mother heard you tell the jokes you tell us?

Todd: My mother? Where do you think I get 'em?

More laughter

Carrie: I believe it. Let me tell you one I heard my dad tell my mom.

Mr. Brock looked up from his work.

Mr. Brock: OK, guys, enough playtime. Get to work now.

Students: (protesting) Aw c'mon, Mr. B. Just one more.

Mr. Brock: (smiling) Nope, not now. Get to work.

Melanie glanced at Shonda. Shonda was looking down at her desk. The girls had discussed Todd's jokes and innuendos before. It made them uncomfortable, but oh well, welcome to high school.

Discussion Questions

Discuss and answer the following questions.

1. Was the above incident severe? Explain.
2. Persistent? Explain.

3. Pervasive? Explain.
4. Does it make a difference that the incident took place after school?
5. Only the two sophomore girls seemed to be uncomfortable. Could that have just been because they were the youngest students in the class?
6. Could the incident have been considered sexual harassment if the sophomore girls had not been in the class?
7. How do you determine if an action is unwelcome or not?
8. If no students come forth with complaints about Todd's jokes, does that mean he is not sexually harassing others? Could this just be humor in poor taste?
9. What was Mr. Brock's role in the incident? Should he have done something differently?
10. Does the fact that the joke did not degrade either gender make a difference when determining if the action was sexually harassing? Why or why not?

3

What Should Teachers Do about Peer Sexual Harassment?

SCENARIO

Kathy Croft stepped out of her classroom into the hall with about three minutes remaining before the bell rang to signal the start of fifth period. She had eaten her lunch sitting at her desk so she could review a video clip she planned on showing to her next class. Ted Rowley, another eighth-grade science teacher who taught next door to her, was talking to Monica Birch from two doors down the hall.

"Hi Kathy. What's happening? We missed you in the lunch lounge," Monica said.

"Oh, I had some work to do. What were you two laughing about?"

"We were listening to that group of kids standing against the wall over there. The guys were rating each girl's figure as she passed. Ted was just saying how nothing changes. Guys did that when we were in junior high back in the 'old days.'" Monica replied, making quotation signs with her fingers.

"Yeah," Ted joined in. "Except then instead of saying 'You're so hot' or 'There goes a number three,' we said boring things like 'Hey Sexy' or 'Is looking in the mirror a scary thing for you?'"

Kathy looked disgusted. "You're kidding. Were those boys really rating girls' looks?"

"Sure," Monica said, laughing. "Don't get all bothered about it, Kath. They're just being normal thirteen-year-old boys. Remember what that guest speaker told us? Middle school boys think about sex 90 percent of the time."

"That doesn't make it right. It sounds like sexual harassment to me. Someone needs to talk to those boys. Girls don't have to put up with that."

"Oh, get off your high horse, Croft." Ted said. "You sound like a feminist."

"Is there something wrong with that?" Kathy retorted.

"Hey, whoa you two," said Monica. "Don't get all crazy about something that doesn't even matter! Don't you remember being in middle school, Kath?"

Kathy started to reply, but just then the bell rang, and her students started crowding their way into her room. She turned and started greeting them. Later, after her last class was over, Kathy thought back to the conversation with her colleagues. She didn't feel right about the boys' actions. But, after all, she was a first-year teacher, and Ted and Monica seemed to think the boys' actions were harmless. Maybe it wouldn't happen again. Knowing that was a cop-out, Kathy tried to decide if she should tell the eighth-grade counselor about the incident. She decided against it. Better not to make waves the first year in the building. But it still bothered her.

RECOGNIZING THE PROBLEM

Evidence suggests that adults in school settings are doing less than they should to stop peer sexual harassment. Three major reasons for that are:

1. Teachers do not witness the incidents.
2. Students are unwilling to report incidents to teachers.
3. Even when they are aware of sexual harassment incidents, teachers fail to intervene or take corrective action. Even when girls told a teacher or administrator about a harassment incident, nothing happened to the harasser in 45 percent of the incidents reported (NOW Legal Defense and Education Fund, 1999).

With the number of students reporting they have been sexually harassed at over 80 percent, it is safe to assume that many of the incidents are not witnessed by teachers. Though we may be quick to blame teachers for allowing sexual harassment to go on in the school setting, it is difficult to stop something unless you are aware of it.

As many as 90 percent of sexual harassment incidents take place in the hallways outside classrooms (OSSTF, 1994). With the many high schools with populations exceeding 2,000 and even middle and elementary schools containing several hundred students, it is not unrealistic to assume that in a crowded hallway, even with all of the teachers standing in the halls, sexual harassment among peers goes unnoticed.

Secondary students are unsupervised in restrooms, and there are always out-of-the-way areas where students walk without adult supervision. Teachers cannot confront the alleged harassers if they do not know who they are. Additional supervision and heightened teacher awareness of the problem could curtail some of the incidents, but when teachers are not aware of the violations they cannot stop them.

So while it is a correct assumption that many sexual harassment incidents go unnoticed by teachers and other school personnel, that is not to say that teachers are blameless. Certainly incidents that take place in classrooms should be witnessed by teachers and addressed. Likewise, students should always be supervised in common areas and hallways, and incidents that occur in those areas should be addressed when a teacher sees them.

An equally large problem is that when students are harassed, too many times they are unwilling to report the incident to an adult. The AAUW study that included responses from 2,064 students found that only 20 percent of the harassed students reported the incident to a teacher or other school personnel (AAUW, 2001).

But of more concern than that, perhaps, is the number of times that teachers or other school personnel *are* aware of the harassment and do nothing about it or even punish the students who report the harassing. Sexual harassment is being tolerated and overlooked by teachers and administrators (Stein, et al., 1993). The accusers even suffer at the hands of their *teachers* or of their fellow students. Mary Jo McGrath (2007), the California lawyer who has handled a number of such cases, says, "It's brutal what happens to people who complain" (p. 5).

When discussing the 1993 AAUW report on sexual harassment, Yafee goes on to say that "One of the most demoralizing aspects of harassment many students reported, was the lack of support from adults. Students stated than even when teachers and administrators witnessed the harassing behavior, they sometimes declined to intervene or take corrective action" (p. 7). Students often complain that sexual harassment occurs at school and in front of school personnel who ignore it (Fineran, 2002, p. 10).

Students have described being ignored, disbelieved, blamed, and sometimes punished when they report instances of harassment to teachers
and other adults. In the AAUW study, students who said they had been
sexually harassed by peers identified lack of support from adults as one
of the most demoralizing aspects of the harassment. Students stated that
even when teachers and administrators witnessed the harassing behavior, they sometimes declined to intervene or take corrective action.
(Stone & Couch, 2004, p. 3)

However, research suggests that five years after the AAUW report
teachers were more intolerant than earlier toward peer sexual harassment issues (Stone & Couch, 2004). We can only hope that that is the
case. Teachers *must* be intolerant of peer sexual harassment. The issue
cannot be dismissed as normal flirting. It cannot be ignored because
school personnel think it is harmless action due to "raging hormones"
or downplayed as only "inappropriate behavior."

THE TEACHERS' RESPONSIBILITY

It is important that teachers have information and training concerning sexual harassment issues among students so they can recognize
problems and will know the proper steps to take to prevent or address
the issues. When a teacher witnesses or suspects that a student is being sexually harassed by another student, the teacher should take im-
mediate action. The teacher needs to understand that the alleged victim must have considered the behavior *unwelcome*.

Most school policies require that the teacher immediately report the
incident to the appropriate school administrator. In less serious offenses the harasser may first be confronted by the teacher in private
and told that the action is not acceptable and will not be tolerated.
The conversation with the alleged harasser may include the following
questions: (1) "Are you familiar with the sexual harassment policy?"
(2) "Did you realize that your actions fell under the definition of sexual harassment?" and the following comments:

"Those were not harmless comments (or actions). They were very
hurtful, and they will not be tolerated in this classroom or anywhere
on this campus." "Humiliating a peer is wrong and will lead to your
being disciplined. I am sending you to talk with _____ " (the appropriate school official designated in the policy).

The victim needs to be assured immediately that the school will not take the incident lightly, and that something will be done. There are too many reports like these from victims:

> "Adults watched, students appealed for help, and the adults offered only innocuous and insipid solutions" (Stein, 1995, p. 154).
> "In science class, the boys snap our bras. The teacher doesn't really care. He doesn't say anything. . . . the boys just laugh." (Shakeshift et al., 1995, p. 42 as reported by Koepels & Dupper, 1999)

Conversation with the victim should include the following questions: "Has _____ said (or done) this to you before today?" "How often?" "Where does this usually occur?" "Have you ever reported the remarks (or actions) to a teacher or counselor?" and the following remarks: "What _____ said (or did) to you was unacceptable and against school policy. I am sorry it happened, and I will take steps to prevent it from ever happening again."

At the very least the harasser needs to acknowledge his/her wrongdoing and apologize to the victim, and the teacher needs to document the incident and report it to the school counselor and the administrator in charge of discipline and/or the school compliance officer in charge of discrimination violations. Those people will contact the parents and proceed with the investigation.

Documentation by the teacher should follow the guidelines in the school's sexual harassment policy. If there is no policy, or if it is weak, the teacher should be sure the documentation includes the names of the students involved, both alleged harasser and victim, the time and date of the incident, who reported the incident, and exact details of the incident, including direct quotes from the participants. The teacher should make a copy of the documentation and file it in a locked cabinet and then turn the original over to the administrators.

Depending on school district policy, in less serious cases the teacher may be the one who calls the parents of the harasser and the parent of the victim to tell them about the incident and what steps the school is taking to prevent it from happening again. An example of a case like this would be a fifth-grade girl taunting a male classmate by calling him a "sissy" and asking him if he had ruffles on his underwear. The teacher may choose to handle a seemingly minor incident like that by herself, talking to both of the students and documenting the incident.

If the teacher does contact the parents of both children involved, she/he should be aware that either or both sets of parents may be hostile when they hear about the incident. If the conversation is not satisfactory, an administrator should be assigned to communicate with the parents.

In all cases the teacher should document the action and the discussion. If the incident occurred in the classroom the harasser should be separated from the victim. This may mean a change in the seating arrangement or, depending upon the seriousness of the incident, changing the schedule of one of the students. No student should be required to be around another student who has sexually harassed her or him.

What teachers should *not* do is ignore the incident or make light of it. With the exception of the compliance officer or the appropriate administrator, the teacher should not discuss the incident with others in the building unless it is in the best interest of the students involved. Sexual harassment is serious; it should not be fodder for gossip.

After the teacher has reported the incident to the proper administrators, he or she should continue to follow the school policy. That may mean retaining copies of the documentation concerning the incident, or meeting with the administrator(s) and parents for further discussion.

Victims Who Are Reluctant to Confront Their Alleged Harasser

If a teacher did not witness the sexual harassment, but a student confides in her/him, it is very important that the student knows at the beginning that if the teacher concludes that the student was indeed sexually harassed, action will be taken. Sometimes students are reluctant for the story to go any further than the teacher because of possible repercussions from other students. It is important that students are able to trust teachers in whom they confide, so it is critical that the teacher can convince the victim that the action must be stopped, and that she/he will be protected as much as possible.

Serious cases involving sexual assault would of course have to be reported to law enforcement agencies even without a complaint from the student. In any case, the teachers must consider whether the incidents are affecting or did affect other students. If so, action must be taken to protect other students from being harassed as well as the student who confides in the teacher. The teacher should seek advice from the school counselor without revealing the students' names.

Teachers and other school personnel must use their judgment and common sense to determine actions to take, always following school policy. In all cases they must act as moral, compassionate employees who have the best interests of the students at heart and who follow the school rules and guidelines. As always when making decisions that affect students, the question must be "What is best for the student?"

Suspected sexual harassment by students should never be ignored. Teachers should always be on the lookout for incidents. If the teacher is not sure if the incident is sexual harassment, she/he should talk to a counselor or the sexual harassment compliance officer. If a teacher witnesses harassing, she should immediately speak with the students involved and document the incident and conversation. All incidents should be reported to the appropriate administrator.

Teachers must know the definition of sexual harassment based on hostile environment. They also need to know what the school or district policy is concerning peer sexual harassment and the name of the person to whom they should report suspected incidents of sexual harassment. All suspected incidents must be well documented and handled immediately. In mild cases such as a onetime teasing, the teacher may choose to contact the participants and parents himself or herself. Documentation is still necessary.

One last comment—a study conducted among Brazilian high school students concluded that teacher norms such as taking actions to curb such behaviors had no direct correlation with sexual harassment or its frequency. Possible explanations included overall school climate and lack of support from administrators (Anderson, 2006). What schools can do to prevent sexual harassment will be discussed in a later chapter.

CASE STUDY

Directions: Read the following case study. Answer the questions following the study.

Background

Almond Middle School is located in a small Midwestern community with a population of approximately 7,000 people. The middle school has 600 students in grades six to eight. The principal, assistant principal, and school counselor are all males. The school district has never been involved in litigation.

The Participants

Susan Jones, a first-year teacher who teaches seventh grade at Almond.

Becky Kraft, a seventh-grade girl who makes average grades and has never been in trouble at school.

Todd Green, an eighth-grade boy who is an average student and popular with his peers

Other eighth-grade boys, including Matt Lawson, a "nice kid."

Seventh-grade girls.

Incident

Susan Jones was putting her student papers into her briefcase and getting ready to go home. It had been a long week, the last one before spring break, but today was finally Friday. Yea! She couldn't wait to leave her job behind her for a few days. Just as she finished clearing off her desk, Becky Kraft came through the door.

"May I talk to you a minute, Ms. Jones?"

"Of course, Becky, but why aren't you on the bus?"

"My mom is picking me up, and she called the office and told them she would be late."

"OK. What's on your mind?"

Becky looked down at her feet: "Something has been happening. It's really embarrassing. I don't know how to say this."

"Hmmm. Is this something that is happening at home?"

"No. It happens at school, and it's really gross."

"OK," Susan said. "Have you told your parents? Did it happen today?"

"Yes, it happened today. I haven't told my folks. My dad would get so mad he would do something stupid that would really embarrass me, and my friends would be angry."

Susan sat silently for a moment. "Becky, you can trust me not to tell your parents unless this is something that is hurting you. But would you rather talk to Mr. Borger, the school counselor?"

Becky looked up in panic. "No! I could never tell a man what is happening!"

Slightly alarmed, Susan walked around her desk and put her arm around Becky. "OK. Why don't you start at the beginning and tell me what's going on. We can decide together what should be done about it."

Becky sighed. "All right. Right after Christmas when we came back to school Todd Green walked up to me and grabbed hold of his . . . his . . ." Becky looked at the floor and stopped talking.

"His crotch?" Susan asked gently.

"Yeah. That's right. His crotch," Becky said, relieved.

"Were his pants unzipped, Becky?" asked Susan.

"No."

"Did he say anything?"

"No. Not that time."

"So it happened again?"

"Yeah. He did it a lot of times. Not just to me, either. Then he started saying really awful things."

Susan patted Becky's arm." Like what, Becky?"

"Like 'I want you to suck my . . .'" Becky choked back a sob.

Susan sighed. Nothing in her teacher ed classes had prepared her to deal with situations like this. "Did anyone else hear this?"

"Oh yes." Becky finally looked up. "He said it to a lot of girls, and that's not all. Pretty soon a whole lot of the fifth-grade boys and even some of the sixth-grade boys were grabbing their . . . you know, and saying things like that. Now they do it all the time except when a teacher is around."

"So what do the other girls think of this?" Susan asked.

"Well," said Becky quietly, "One of the sixth-grade girls told my friends and me that we were just babies who probably didn't understand what the boys were talking about anyway. Mostly the girls in my class try to not look, and pretend not to hear the boys. Even Matt Lawson said it the other day. You know him, Ms. Jones. He's really nice. He was standing by Todd and when Todd said those bad things, Matt said it too! He didn't laugh or anything like the other boys. He looked kinda uncomfortable. But he said them anyway."

"OK," Susan said. "Let me talk to Mr. Carter and Mr.—"

"No!" Becky yelled. "You can't tell anyone! Everyone would be mad at me!"

"OK, OK," Susan said quickly. "Let me think about what to do. In the meantime, it would be a good idea for you to tell your parents."

Becky looked very unhappy. "Please, please don't tell anyone I told you, Ms. Jones. I have to see if my mom is here." Becky ran from the room.

Susan slumped down in her chair. Great. She had just told a student they could work something out, and now she didn't know who to talk to about the problem. She really didn't want to lose Becky's trust, but shouldn't she do something? She would think about it over spring break. Maybe the boys would forget about it after being away from school for nine days.

Discussion Questions:

1. Were the boys' actions severe? How did you make that determination?
2. Is there evidence that the incidents occurred persistently?
3. Were the incidents pervasive? How do you know?
4. What students were being affected by the actions?
5. Does it make a difference that no other students had come forth with a complaint?
6. Could this be a case of sexual harassment even if none of the girls' grades had been affected by the incidents?
7. Is it possible that some of the girls were being harassed, but that others who witnessed the incidents were *not* being harassed?
8. Was this a case of sexual harassment? If not, why not? If so, were any students other than Becky being harassed? If so, who? What evidence do you have to support your conclusions?

4

What Is the School Counselor's Role?

Bethany sat outside the tenth-grade counselor's office with her chin resting on her chest. She was trying to decide if this was really what she wanted to do when the counselor called her name.

"Hello Bethany. I'm Ms. Jackson. What can I do for you today?" She smiled at Bethany as she noticed the hesitation on the girl's face.

Bethany looked up. The woman looked OK. Kinda old though. What if she thought Bethany was just a baby? What if she thought she was lying?

"Hi. My friends said I should come in and talk to you. I dunno, though. Maybe I should come back another time. I probably should get back to PE class," Bethany said shyly.

"Whatever you think, Bethany," Ms. Jackson said. She smiled and continued. "But since you already have a pass from class and I freed up time for us to visit, why don't we relax for a few minutes? I've been planning to touch base with each of the sophomore girls soon."

Bethany thought for a moment. If she went back to class she would have to change clothes, and she would barely have time to get on the court before the first bell rang. Of course she could just leave and hang out in the locker room until class was over. Before she could make a decision, Ms. Jackson continued.

"I looked up your records when I received your request for an appointment form. You're a really good student. Is this about a class?"

Ms. Jackson stepped aside and Bethany reluctantly went on into her office. The counselor motioned her into a chair and sat in a chair beside her. As soon as they were both seated Bethany started to say something, but to her dismay she burst into tears. Ms. Jackson didn't say anything until the sobs had subsided a little.

"Tell me about the tears," Ms. Jackson said softly.

Bethany hung her head. "I am so embarrassed. I never cry! It's not like I'm one of those dumb girls that weeps all the time about losing her boyfriend or not having a date for some stupid party. I can't believe I'm crying! I am so sorry."

"Hey, don't be," Ms. Jackson said. "What you feel is important."

"Maybe," Beth said, her head still down. "But if some stupid boy saw me he'd probably say, 'Look out, Harper is PMSing.' I hate that. They're heartless insensitive dorks!"

The counselor smiled. "I'm here to listen if you want to talk about it. Is it one of those 'heartless insensitive dorks' that is making your life miserable right now?"

Beth smiled a little. "Yeah. But not just right now. It's been going on all semester. I thought surely he would let up, but now I'm just sick and tired of it all. Kara said I should tell you about it. I've never talked to a counselor before, though. I don't know what to say."

"I'm listening."

Beth hesitated, looking as if she were having a discussion with herself. "OK," she said finally, "but please don't tell anyone I told you."

Ms. Jackson pursed her lips for a second. "Beth, as a counselor I need to follow a model of confidentiality. That means that if you or anyone else is in danger I will have to tell someone."

"I don't know if it's hurting anyone else, but if it got out that I told you, it would hurt me! Maybe I just better go and forget all about it." Beth said, rising.

"I'll tell you what," Ms. Jackson said. "Why don't you tell me about the big picture of the problem without mentioning names, and we can take it from there?"

"I guess. But I don't want it spread all over school that I came in here. Sometimes this boy does this stuff in the class we have together and the teacher just ignores it. The other boys already laugh at me."

"I will not discuss what you tell me with any other students, Beth. Do you want to tell me what has been going on?"

"Well, when we came back from Christmas break we had a new kid in the sophomore class. He's in two of my classes. All of my friends think he's cute, but I hate him!" Beth looked down at her hands.

"Go on."

"He's always brushing up against me and saying 'Sorry' with a smirk. The past two weeks he's been putting his hand under my shirt! When I tell him to stop, the other guys in the class laugh, and he winks at me. Then today when I was working on my lab project he came up and unhooked my bra and touched me! Keith Thomas was standing there and he just hooted! I was so embarrassed I ran to the restroom, and when I came back my teacher yelled at me for leaving. When I said I didn't want to work next to T . . . to this boy, my teacher just said that the lab sites were set up for the whole term and I just needed to stay away from the boys. She sounded like it was all my fault. I was so mad. Then I got a copy of my midterm grades and my grades in three classes are lower than I've ever had! This is just a horrible day! I wish I could go home and never come back!"

COUNSELORS' ROLES

Because of their training in mental health issues and social problems, school counselors should have a big role to play in the elimination of peer sexual harassment. In fact they are probably the best-qualified school personnel to develop a plan and educate the school personnel and the students concerning peer sexual harassment. Peer sexual harassment incidents are not isolated problems in a school. Stein (1995) echoes the sentiments of most observers when she says that a school culture of sexual harassment exists in a wide and troubling social context. The bigger problem is the climates of schools that allow sexual discrimination; schools in which incidents of sexual harassment are common and accepted as "just part of growing up."

School personnel cannot solve the problem of kids being bombarded with sexual issues from the media, online, in computer games, in fashion, and almost everywhere they turn. They can, however, strive to help make school a safe place—a place of learning, not of intimidation and fear. That is where school counselors come into the picture. Whether it is setting up peer counseling groups, building a schoolwide plan for preventing peer sexual harassment, or educating students and staff on the issues, the expertise of school counselors can play a huge role in combating peer sexual harassment. Their input into policy development and revision should be valued by administrators.

Rowe (1996) reported over a decade ago that school counselors had begun to see an increase in the number of students who were coming to them to talk about being harassed by their peers. The counselors expressed needs including knowledge of how to follow through with allegations of harassment, how to prevent it, how to help students assert themselves, and how to work with parents and other school personnel concerning peer sexual harassment. Since then the numbers have increased; the needs of the counselors are the same. Counselors and other school personnel need to be proactive when dealing with peer sexual harassment. Too many children and youth are being hurt by that phenomenon. We need to prevent it, not pick up the pieces after an incident.

Although the public and even many teachers may think that school counselors spend their time counseling students, the fact is that counselors have so many other responsibilities that counseling students or student groups is many times a small part of their job. Particularly in secondary school, counselors spend a huge percentage of their time arranging student schedules. Some counselors work full-time doing career counseling. In other schools, counselors deal with discipline issues.

All of those duties are important, but counselors have not been trained to schedule classes, nor should they ever be in charge of discipline. Career counseling is a legitimate role for a counselor, but it should not be her/his only obligation. Students seeing counselors in these roles get the wrong idea about the role of the counselor and when incidents arise for which they need counseling they are reluctant to go to the school counselor for help.

School counselors run into many roadblocks when they try to help students who have been sexually harassed. The first problem is that the majority of the students do not tell any school official about the incident(s). The counselors cannot assist students when they do not know what the students' needs are. The second problem is that when students do share with the counselor about a harassment situation, many times the students only do so when the counselor assures them that the story will go no further, and that is not realistic in serious situations. Often the student is not willing for the counselor to share information with anyone else, including parents, and is afraid for the alleged harasser(s) to be confronted.

When that happens, the ethical and legal obligations of the counselors conflict with their desire to gain the trust of the students. Once a counselor, teacher, administrator, or other school official becomes aware that a student is being sexually harassed, he/she has an obligation to act on the matter. Failure to do so could result in the school being liable in a lawsuit. This was established in *Davis v. Monroe County Bd. of Education* (1999) and will be discussed in detail in chapter 6.

However, once a counselor betrays a student's trust, the counselor may lose that trust, and the student may very well refuse to talk with the counselor further. The counselor has the often difficult task of negotiating between discerning the maturity level of minors and their confidentiality needs and addressing the parents' rights to be aware of the critical issues facing their child.

The Code of Ethics and Standards of Practice of both the American Counseling Association (ACA, 2005) and the American School Counselor Association (ASCA, 2004) instructs school counselors to protect the privacy of students unless disclosure to another party is in the student's best interest or is required by law. That requires good judgment on the counselor's part. The law and school policies require the counselor to report the sexual harassment. "A school has actual notice of sexual harassment if an agent or responsible employee of the school receives notification" (OCR, 1997, p. 12037).

School or district policy should clearly state that sexual harassment incidents must be reported to the appropriate administrator and it must be understood by counselors that reporting is not optional. That is one decision they do not have to make.

Stone (2000) reminds us that the Office of Civil Rights does recognize that declining to honor a student's confidentiality may discourage reporting of sexual harassment. The OCR also recognizes that withholding the alleged victim's name may infringe on the rights of the alleged harasser. The OCR suggests that a balance must be struck to honor the victim's request for confidentiality if that can be done "consistently with the school's obligation to remedy the harassment and take steps to prevent further harassment" (OCR, Sexual Harassment Policy Guidance, 1997, p. 12037).

What, then, is the role and responsibility of the school counselor? The counselor must at all times act in the best interest of the student while following the legal and ethical guidelines required. Determining the student's best interest as to what other actions to take is the area where the education and expertise of the counselor comes into play.

The counselor must make that call based on her/his experience, knowledge of the student, and ethical considerations. If the victim's insistence on anonymity continues, it may not be possible to proceed with actions against the accused harasser. If however, the victim is being stalked or is in danger or the harassment does not stop, then the counselor will need to disclose the victim's name to the proper authority. School counselors have a duty to warn and protect minor clients and others if danger exists.

Counselors need to know how to deal with situations like Bethany's dilemma in the scenario above so they will not have to spend time figuring out solutions but can counsel the student wisely following legal and ethical guidelines. The counselor needs to determine if her/his role is as a listener/counselor only, or if it should be that of an advocate for the student.

A PLAN OF ACTION

In order for the counselor to make effective decisions it is important that a comprehensive plan is in place for counselors and other school personnel to follow in addition to the school policy.

That plan needs to be developed *by* counselors and *for* counselors with input from parents and administrators as well. One additional advantage to including parents and administrators is that such meetings raise the level of awareness among those groups. This may be accomplished by using a school counseling parent advisory committee that includes parents who give the counseling team ideas on the school counseling program.

The peer sexual harassment plan should include the legal guidelines and actions listed in the sexual harassment policy of the school or district, and then it should be tailored specifically to counselors and should outline the steps to be taken with the student when incidents occur. The plan needs to include guidelines to follow when students are reporting incidents they have witnessed as well as when students are reporting harassment in which they have been the victims. The plan, developed by counselors and other personnel, is more than just a policy.

A comprehensive plan should include the following:

1. A method to educate all school personnel on the prevalence and consequences of sexual harassment and how to prevent and address it
2. A method to educate the students on the definition and prevention of peer sexual harassment

3. Specific components to include when counseling alleged victims and alleged peer harassers
4. A follow-up process to ensure that students and school personnel are constantly aware of how to deal with sexual harassment

Once such a plan is in place it is imperative that all counselors in the school or district are aware of it and that they understand their roles as outlined in the plan. Of course the conversations that actually take place between the counselor and student, the counselor and parents, and/or the counselors and the alleged harassers will depend on the circumstances and will be up to the discretion of the counselor, who is the professional with the expertise and education to make those decisions.

THE EDUCATING ROLE OF
THE SCHOOL COUNSELOR

As with any problem that affects a school, it is much better to prevent unwanted incidents than to take care of them later. In the matter of sexual harassment in school, it goes beyond being "better" to being crucial. The aftereffects of being sexually harassed range from poor grades and emotional scars to depression, dropping out of school, and even suicide. Yaffee (1995) reported on a follow-up of three girls who were repeatedly sexually harassed by their peers. Two of them who were then in college reported that they still had deep emotional scars and very often felt weary and hopeless. The third girl committed suicide while grasping her teddy bear. Unfortunately these stories are not uncommon. It is not enough to punish the offenders and counsel the victims. We must concentrate on *preventing* peer sexual harassment.

School counselors are probably the best-equipped school personnel to take the lead in setting up programs to prevent peer sexual harassment. It is important when initiating a program that counselors are aware of current laws and policies. Those laws will be discussed later in this book. If counselors have questions not addressed in that chapter they should consult the district's legal advisor.

As stated previously, every school/district must have a policy in place that addresses sexual harassment. Suggestions for writing and implementing such a policy as well as sample policies will be found in chapter 7.

Educating School Personnel

The authors of the plan need to be sure that participants include personnel other than just teachers and administrators. Custodians, administrative assistants, cafeteria workers, school resource officers, and paraprofessionals and aides need to know how to deal with sexual harassment issues.

A presentation at a required workshop would be one method that could be used to accomplish this. The counselor(s) could present definitions of sexual harassment along with handouts for the participants to keep. It is not enough, however, just to *present* the information; it must be *taught*. In other words, the participants should be checked for understanding and then assessed on their knowledge of the subject and what actions should be taken.

The leader should be sure to use visuals such as a PowerPoint presentation or transparencies so the visual learners will be able to retain the information. Role-playing several scenarios to determine which are examples of sexual harassment would further reinforce the material.

Three points need to be emphasized in the workshop:

- Peer sexual harassment is harmful to all students, with sometimes tragic results.
- Peer sexual harassment will not be tolerated.
- Peer sexual harassment prevents learning.

In addition, the following *skills* should be emphasized:

- Skills in the identification of peer sexual harassment—where does teasing end and harassment begin?
- Skills for implementing a "no tolerance" policy for peer sexual harassment
- Skills for dealing with sexual harassment complaints from alleged victims and parents
- Skills for dealing with alleged harassers and parents

These last two skills will be necessary for counselors, but teachers should also be aware of how to talk with students who harass others and if necessary to their parents.

Following the instruction, faculty should break up into small groups and be given three or four scenarios to discuss to determine if the incidents are sexual harassment, and if so, what action should be taken according to district policy. Finally, the participants should be assessed on their knowledge by completing a short individual quiz. The quiz should also present scenarios and give participants options as to what choices to make in each situation.

It is important for teachers and other school personnel to know at this point that they need to do more than just report harassment incidents to the compliance office, though that is required. They need to be on the lookout constantly for incidents of sexual harassment. They need to be confident enough to reassure students that sexual harassment is not acceptable and that it will not be tolerated.

Educating Students

Learning takes place in a nurturing, positive school environment. It is the responsibility of administrators, teachers, counselors, and social workers to ensure that the school climate is conducive to learning. Students cannot learn when they are fearful, embarrassed, or uncomfortable. A student spends over thirty hours per week at school. How sad it would be to be in an uncomfortable or dangerous environment that often! Too often survival, not learning, is the primary objective of students who are constantly harassed. So how can school personnel change that?

Many school districts include a statement on sexual harassment or bullying in their student handbooks. The students are instructed to read the handbook and sign a statement confirming that they have read it, and in some districts have shared the information with their parents. We are being naive if we think that is actually happening in most cases. Too often parents don't even see the handbook, and students sign the paper without reading any of the information. Even if every teacher went over the information the first day of school, that is not enough. How presumptuous of educators to think that reading a rule to a child or adolescent will prevent an injustice!

Ideally counselors would be able to go into each classroom and teach the students what to do if they think they are victims of sexual harassment and how to prevent sexual harassment. Unfortunately many schools are too large for counselors to get around to every classroom. An alternative would be for them to talk to 100 or fewer students at a time in a common setting. This would require a commitment from the administrators and staff. That sounds unrealistic when teachers are already burdened with too much to accomplish in too short a time and have too many days taken out of the teaching schedule. But if the teachers can understand that *as harassment decreases, learning increases,* they should be more willing to give up one class period a year.

Just telling students about sexual harassment is not enough. They need to be impressed with what it is, the difference between flirting and harassment, and what they should do when they think they are being harassed. Role playing is an excellent tool for educating students on the difference between flirting and bullying or harassment. However, because role playing is sometimes uncomfortable for middle school students, the actors for that age group could be the counselors or other adults. At other levels, the student leaders could and should take an active part in helping with the workshops. The counselors need to be sure the students are taking the responsibility seriously; peer sexual harassment is not a joke.

An alternative to role playing would be for students to be videotaped earlier acting out the scenarios. Like in the workshops for the teachers, students should always be checked for understanding. This could be done by presenting them with several scenarios and having them determine whether or not sexual harassment was involved and what the characters should do about it. With some age groups this could be accomplished in small group discussion. In others, when the students are just not mature enough to discuss sexual issues with their peers, it should be done individually. But however it is handled, the facilitators (counselors and teacher helpers) must be sure that every student who walks out the door understands that sexual harassment is no laughing matter and will not be tolerated.

Developing a plan may seem like a daunting task to already overworked school counselors and administrators and teacher leaders. When they are aware of the negative effects that peer sexual harassment has on learning and on the mental and emotional health of students, they should make it a priority. They do not, however, have to start from scratch. There are several programs available to help students and school personnel understand and address the issue. As Yaffe (1995) reported over a decade ago:

> There is no shortage of published and filmed materials designed to help students, teachers and others become better equipped to deal with these changing times. There are prepared curricula and handbooks containing

a wealth of information . . . lesson plans, overheads, scenarios for role-playing exercises, first person accounts of actual incidents, newspaper clipping, quizzes to uncover preconceptions and misinformation and videos that attempt to give the sense and feel of the issue. (p. 12)

It is a good idea to look at a curriculum that has been developed by others, but I strongly recommend that school counselors who are charged with educating students about sexual harassment write their own curriculum. School counselors are trained in dealing with mental health and social issues, and they know their particular student population and parents.

The same advice applies to those writing material for training sessions with faculty and staff. The school counselors will best know their own faculty and what training format would be most acceptable to the faculty and staff. Some curricula for students they might want to review *for ideas* include three that have been developed and utilized in Canada:

Sexual Harassment: Intermediate Curriculum
Sexual Harassment in Schools: Recognize It, Prevent It, Stop It
The Joke's Over: Student-to-Student Sexual Harassment in Secondary Schools.

These three programs can be obtained from www.ucalgary.ca/resolve/violenceprevention/English/reviewprog/harassprogs.htm#prog1.

In addition, the National School Boards Association (1996) has produced a video training program worthy of review. A three-session curriculum written by Sousa, Bancroft, and German (1986) is another source. Strauss and Epselan (1992) wrote a curriculum for use with students ages seven to twelve that would be a source for secondary counselors.

Writing The Curriculum for Educating School Personnel

Whether counselors choose to adapt a commercial curriculum or to write their own from scratch, they should be sure that the curriculum includes at a minimum the following:

1. *Rationale.* This should be a paragraph or two explaining why the lessons are necessary and what the facilitators hope to accomplish.

It is important that it be written in age-appropriate language. Peer sexual harassment is very prevalent at the middle school level, and that age group has a tendency either to be uncomfortable with the subject of sex or find it a source of hilarity. The rationale could include a very brief introduction such as "What should you say to your friend David when he says 'I dare you to snap Rita's bra'?" or "How does it make you feel when a boy tells you he likes to look at your boobs?" or "How does it make you feel when another guy calls you 'gay'"

The questions should be followed by the rationale for the lessons. According to the age group, this might include statistics or even a video, but whatever method is used to introduce the rationale, it should clearly explain why the instruction is taking place. For teachers a question might be: "What's wrong with boys rating girls' appearance; hasn't that always gone on in schools?" followed by the reason for the training.

2. *Objectives*. Example: "The participants will be able to define and recognize sexual harassment," or "The participants will be able to list verbally and in writing the steps to be taken when they encounter peer sexual harassment."

3. *Activities*. These may include videos, role playing, small and large group discussion, guest speakers, short information lectures (probably least effective), or assimilation activities. Obviously this will be the part of the plan that is most time-consuming to write. The counselor and the writing committee should put lots of thought into writing the activities so that they are not just time fillers, but interesting and informative activities that will fulfill the objectives.

4. *Assessment*. This step is crucial so the facilitator can find out what the participants actually learned. If they didn't understand, the information will need to be retaught. The facilitator should periodically check for understanding informally during the lesson by questioning and listening to the participants.

Of course the lesson plans for students will be different from the plans for faculty training. It is very important that in both situations the information is presented in an organized manner by someone who is passionate about the subject. Neither faculty nor students should be allowed to treat peer sexual harassment as a laughing matter. For that reason as well as others, it is important that the counselor and the group working on the plans communicate with the administrators, making this topic a priority. It is critical that the counselors and other personnel who develop the plan have input from teachers at all grade levels and even students, so that the activities will be age-appropriate.

Plans for teaching students and school personnel will vary, but at the very least each plan must contain definitions of peer sexual harassment and examples of it. They must also contain information instructing the participants, whether student or school personnel, what action to take.

Specific Information Students Need

Counselors are trained in the best ways to communicate with students. They will know the appropriate methods to use in specific situations. Sometimes this will include individual counseling and other times a group session may be most effective. In any case, an awareness of the rights of others as well as communication and assertiveness training for victims of peer sexual harassment will be necessary. When dealing with students who think they are being sexually harassed by their classmates, the counselors should give them the following information:

- They can and should tell the offender to stop if they are comfortable doing so.
- They should not ignore the harassment. That sounds easier than it is in most cases, as sexual harassment is a play for power on the part of the harasser.
- They can and should talk it over with an adult.
- The school will take the allegations seriously and will protect the student's privacy as much as possible under the law.

All students, including those who are being counseled for committing act of sexual harassment, should be informed that:

- The school *will* take the allegation seriously. They do not have a right to harass any other student; all have a right to be treated with respect.
- Nobody has a right to make another person's life miserable.
- The discipline measures outlined in the school policy *will* be implemented.

The students should be reminded of the peer sexual harassment policy and should be given a copy of it following the discussions.

The counselor should always follow up to see what if anything changed for the student. Other counseling sessions may be required for the mental and emotional health of the student as well as for the counselor to be assured that the unacceptable action has stopped. In serious cases, students may need to be referred to other health professionals who deal with sexual victimization and trauma.

The alleged harasser also needs counseling. This may be as simple as explaining to the student (and the parents) exactly what constitutes sexual harassment and unwelcomeness. In other cases the problem may go deeper and the student may need long-term counseling dealing with such issues as bullying, aggressive behavior, or problems in the student's background (like sexual abuse) that led to the harassment. Once again, the counselor needs to be aware of when another professional should be consulted.

A Follow-Up Plan

Finally, the plan must include suggestions as to how to follow up after the faculty, staff, and students have been educated regarding peer sexual harassment. It would be a good idea for everyone in the schools to receive refresher brochures reminding them to take these issues seriously and what steps to take to report incidents. Knowing, though, that teachers' mailboxes and students' backpacks are crammed with materials at the beginning of a school year, this should be done after the first few weeks of school.

Faculty meetings as well as homerooms are good places to dispense information. It is important that the person in charge has the trust of the faculty and/or students and that the matter will be taken seriously.

Another suggestion is for school walls to feature posters reminding all that peer sexual harassment will not be tolerated. Teachers must support that, or all of the efforts of the educators for the issue will be in vain and the program will be undermined.

SUGGESTIONS FOR SCHOOL COUNSELORS

School counselors must stay current on laws and policies that govern the district as well as ethical standards. If they need help interpreting the law or have questions about ethics, they should ask their supervisor or another counselor who does understand the laws and ethical guidelines The issue of peer sexual harassment is too important to guess at what is correct and acceptable.

Counselors should continually participate in professional development. They need to stay up to date by attending conferences and reading literature on the subject. In addition to the above outline for a plan, they should be at the forefront in *adopting* the plan of action to inform students and staff of sexual harassment issues. They need to encourage teachers to include information on peer sexual harassment where it is appropriate in the curriculum.

School counselors are the best-equipped personnel to deal with sexual harassment issues in the school setting. They need to work with administrators, parents, and other personnel to develop and implement a plan of prevention for the school.

Discussion Questions

Referring to the scenario at the beginning of this chapter, answer the following questions to check your understanding of peer sexual harassment issues.

1. Was it acceptable for the counselor to encourage Bethany to come into her office when Bethany was somewhat reluctant to do so?
2. It would probably not be difficult for the counselor to identify the alleged harasser, as he was a new student in a lab class of a male science teacher, which would narrow the choices. Given that, when the counselor said, "I will not discuss what you tell me with other students," do you think she meant she wouldn't confront the alleged harasser? If so, is that what she should have said?
3. What steps should the counselor take next?
4. Does it make any difference that Bethany's grades have been slipping?
5. What actions if any should be taken in regard to the teacher?
6. Should the counselor call the parents?
7. Do the ages of the students, that is, high school as opposed to grade school or middle school students, make any difference as to how the situation is handled?

5

Preventing Peer Sexual Harassment of Lesbian, Gay, Bisexual, and Transgender Students

SCENARIO

Kevin grabbed his books and dashed out the door of his science class. Sometimes he could make it to his next class without being seen by any of "them " Kevin's friend, Brandon had another name for "them"—He called the gay bashers and bullies "FBI agents—Freakin' Bigoted Idiots." Not to their faces, of course. Brandon could be so funny, but he never laughed when the "FBI goons" made fun of Kevin because they thought he was gay. How ironic; Kevin wasn't gay, but Brandon was! Nobody in the school suspected that their star wrestler was gay, but because his best friend, Kevin, was too shy to ask a girl for a date, didn't play sports, and excelled in choir and art, he had been teased and taunted since sixth grade.

Lately the taunting had turned nastier. When he was walking home from school yesterday two of the football players grabbed him, pulled down his jeans, and stuck a sticky note on his underwear with a derogatory question on it. Two girls from his biology class had witnessed the incident, and Kevin was mortified. The news must have gotten around the school because Sylvia, whom all the kids knew was a lesbian, walked up to Kevin the next morning and told him he should report the incident to the counselor or principal.

Instead, Kevin told Brandon, thinking maybe his friend would give him some advice. He did—his advice was to ignore the kids as usual. But Kevin was tired of it all. He wasn't even gay and his best friend, who was, would not admit it to anyone but Kevin, and would not even stand up for him. On top of that, Kevin's cousin had just moved into the district and would be enrolling tomorrow. All he needed to complicate his life was for his parents or other relatives to hear rumors about his sexual identity! The men in his family already thought he was odd for not being involved in sports.

Kevin had just slid into his seat in math when he was handed a note from his teacher. The eleventh-grade counselor wanted to see him right now. "Wonderful," Kevin thought. Chances are this was not about his schedule. The counselor probably wanted to encourage him to confront his harassers. Kevin heard that was the usual method of handling things when students harassed other students. "Talk about life getting worse," he thought. With that thought in mind, Kevin picked up his books and walked out of class. Walking down the hall trying to decide whether to head to the counselor's office or just keep right on walking out the door, he heard his name called, followed by "Hey fag, who let you out? Are you roaming the halls looking for other 'little girls'?"

All students have constitutional rights to equal protection and are protected under Title IX of the federal Education Amendments Act of 1972 from sex discrimination in educational programs that receive federal funds. That includes lesbian, gay, bisexual, and transgender (LGBT) students and *suspected* LGBT students as well. The harassment of those students must not be ignored just because school personnel or students may think that LGBT students should expect to be harassed because of their sexual orientation. Anecdotal evidence suggests that harassment of lesbian, gay, or bisexual students is often especially heinous. The above scenario is actually mild in contrast to many reports from students. Consider the following quotes:

> I have experienced all forms of harassment and discrimination in school, from verbal and emotional to extreme violence. I have had my teachers join their students in mocking LGBT students. . . . I have been hospitalized because I was beat so bad . . . it's a very, very hostile climate. (Sarah Stuebner as cited in O'Shaughnessy et al., 2004).

Or:

> People kept coming up to me and making fun of me. They would call me horrible names and I would cry all the time. Letters were put in my locker saying things about AIDS and how my parents shouldn't have had me and how I should just die. Kids would threaten me after school and

follow me home yelling things at me. No one should have to go through what I went through at school. (Rhode Island Task Force on Gay and Lesbian Youth, 1996)

Or:

"I'd hear 'faggot' and people would throw things at me. They'd yell at me a lot. One time when the teacher was out of the room, they got in a group and started strangling me with a drafting line. That's about the same consistency as a fishing line. It was so bad that I started to get blood red around my neck, and it cut me." Later in the school year, his classmates also cut him with knives. On another occasion he reports "I was dragged downstairs by my feet."(Human Rights Watch, 2001 as cited in Goldstein, 2001)

Harassment of LGBT students is pervasive and significant. More than that, it is damaging and even life-threatening. In a 2002 survey conducted by the National Mental Health Association (as cited in O'Shaughnessy et al., 2004) 78 percent of the students surveyed reported that students in their school who were gay or thought to be gay are teased or bullied.

Statistics reported in Creating Safe Schools for Gay and Lesbian Students (GLSEN, 1996) include:

- Gay and lesbian youth are two to three times more likely to attempt suicide than heterosexual young people. Suicide is the leading cause of death among those youth.
- Twenty-eight percent of gay and lesbian students in a national study were seen to have dropped out of school because of harassment resulting from their sexual orientation (Remafedi, 1987).
- Forty-five percent of gay males and 20 percent of lesbians report having experienced verbal harassment and/or physical violence as a result of their sexual orientation during high school.
- Depression strikes homosexual youth four to five times more severely than their nongay peers.
- Eighty-one percent of the 900 middle and high school LGBT students who responded to a National School Climate Survey (as cited in Goldstein, 2001) said that faculty or staff rarely intervened when hearing derogatory remarks about LGBT students.

The sexual orientation of these students affects every part of their lives, and dealing with the issues permeates their school days and years. As educators we must address that. Only then can we address the effects these happenings have on learning. It is tremendous. Students, young or old cannot learn in an atmosphere of fear. Until we change the climate for LBGT students, little learning will take place for them.

LEGAL GUIDELINES FOR LGBT STUDENTS

All students have a constitutional right to equal protection under the federal law. Schools have a duty to protect LGBT students from harassment on an equal basis with all other students. If the school fails at this protection, they are liable under the law. The court in a California case in 2000 (*Ray v. Antioch*), found no material difference between a female student being treated as a sex object and a male student insulted and abused due to his harassers' perception that he is a homosexual. Federal district courts in the first, fifth, and eighth circuits have also recognized same-sex peer harassment as actionable under Title IX.

Over a decade ago in *Nabozney v. Podlesny* (1996), the seventh circuit awarded a student $900,000 to settle claims against a Wisconsin school district. The male student had been verbally berated for being gay and had been assaulted numerous times. One time he was pushed into a urinal and urinated on by other male students. Another time he was subjected to a mock rape while students taunted him, saying he should enjoy it. The school had repeatedly been notified about the actions but did not intervene. They should have!

Title IX of the Education Amendment Acts of 1972, while not prohibiting discrimination based on sexual orientation, does prohibit sexual harassment directed at LGBT students if it is sufficiently severe or pervasive. Additionally, the Office of Civil Rights (OCR) Guidelines states specifically,

Although Title IX does not prohibit discrimination on the basis of sexual orientation, sexual harassment directed at gay or lesbian students that is sufficiently serious to limit or deny a student's ability to participate in or benefit from the school's program constitutes sexual harassment prohibited by Title IX. (OCR 2001, § III)

The Guidance, issued by the Department of Education Office of the Office of Civil Rights (2001) clarified their original document, explaining that even if the harasser and the harassed are the same sex, or the victim is gay or lesbian, it may be sexual harassment if the conduct is based on a sexual nature. In other words, if harassing conduct of a sexual nature is directed at a gay or lesbian student it may create a hostile environment. That could constitute a violation of Title IX just as it would for heterosexual students.

Specific Rights of Gay, Lesbian, Bisexual, and Transgender Students

Under federal laws, LGBT students have the following rights:

1. The right to form a Gay, Lesbian, Bisexual, and Transgender student group at school. Under the Equal Access Act and confirmed by *Board of Education of Westside Community Schools v. Mergens* (1990), if a school allows *any* noncurriculuar group to form and meet at the school, then the school must also permit *all* noncurricular groups to meet. This law pertains to secondary schools that receive federal funds if their limited open forum permits even one noncurricular club.

2. The right to express their point of view on LGBT issues. This was established in the landmark case *Tinker v. Des Moines Independent Community School District* (1969), which all educators will recognize as the case involving students who were protesting the U.S. involvement in the Vietnam War by wearing black armbands to class. The *Tinker* case established that students have the right to free speech as long as the speech or conduct does not materially disrupt class work or involve substantial disorder or invasion of the rights of others.

3. The right to post relevant information on a student bulletin board. If the bulletin board is available for use by all groups, the LBGT students must also be allowed to place postings there. Under the First Amendment, the school may regulate time, place, and manner.

4. The right to take a same-gender date to a prom or other school function. Under Title IX, schools are prohibited from discriminating on the basis of sex in its invitation to a prom or other school function. (However, parents may elect to remove their student from sex education curricula containing LBGT material and

the student may be excused from attending the classes without penalty.)

But the most important right that LBGT students have is the right and expectation to attend school in a safe environment free from name-calling and more serious harassment. The phrase "that's so gay" is more than just a comment. It is a put-down of gay students, as is being called a "faggot" whether or not the recipient of the remark is gay. Likewise, the huge number of students who call a girl a "lesbo" when they're teasing a friend are using the term in a derogatory sense and insulting lesbians.

Schools are liable for peer sexual harassment of LBGT students just as they are for all students. Schools are required to have a sexual harassment policy in place, and all students fall under the Equal Protection Clause.

To meet the specific needs of LBGT students, school personnel need to be aware of those needs and vigilant in protecting the rights of these students as well as all of their students. The school mission statement should include a statement acknowledging the importance of respect for all diversities. In their own classrooms or gymnasiums, teachers should establish clearly defined guidelines about intolerance for name-calling or harassment. They should never make assumptions based on sexual orientation or perceived sexual orientation. When the subject of sexual orientation comes up in a class discussion, the teacher should be the role model and treat the subject in a mature, nonbiased way. It is important that bigoted or biased school personnel not be allowed to influence instruction in these areas. That of course does not mean that some teachers will not have beliefs different from the students; just that they do not have the right to force their beliefs on students, nor do they have the right to snicker or make disparaging comments about subjects of which they disapprove.

All school personnel should be encouraged to expand their knowledge about the social difficulties (which lead to academic difficulties) for LBGT students. Administrators, counselors, and social workers should take the lead in informing students and staff (including cooks, custodians, and bus drivers) about the policies and the no-tolerance stance that needs to be taken by the school against those who harass gay, lesbian, bisexual, or transgender students.

CASE STUDY

Background

Lewis High School is one of the four high schools located in a small city in a northeastern state. The student population is around 1,600, and the school has eighty-eight teachers, eight administrators, and four counselors. The student population is 68 percent White, 18 percent Hispanic, 9 percent Black, and 5 percent Black and other. The school has had the same principal for six years. Four years ago there was a serious racial confrontation between Hispanic and White students. At that time two assistant principals were transferred and replaced with female Hispanic administrators.

Participants

Tom Raydon, principal
Betsy Torez, assistant principal
Maria Sanchez, assistant principal
Roger Choiu, assistant principal
Rob Galleger, assistant principal
Susan K., ninth-grade counselor
Terry Jones, tenth-grade counselor
Lynn Norse, eleventh-grade counselor
Jan Hulstead, twelfth-grade counselor
Kyle Jordan, part-time social worker
John Coast, school resource officer

Incident

The weekly meeting of the Administrative Council for the high school is about to begin. Because this is an off-campus in-service day for teachers, the teacher representatives are not present.

Tom Raydon: OK busy people. Let's get this show on the road. We'll dispense with the department reports, as the chairs are not here. Before we discuss the tardy policy changes, is there anything really pressing on your minds?

Lynn Norse: Actually, I have something I think we need to address. In her ninth-grade computer class Donna Cain has something that keeps coming up that really concerns me. There are only four girls in the class of twenty, and it seems the girls are constantly being teased by the boys. She has spoken to the guys several times and even sent a couple of them down to see Roger, but nothing changes. The boys call the girls names like "Babe," "Sugar," and even on occasion "Slut," or "Easy Pickings." Normally I would say this is a problem that needs to be handled by the teacher, but that doesn't seem to work. Maybe they don't take Donna seriously because she is young and attractive herself. The boys think it is funny and one even went so far to say to Donna, "You're a babe yourself, Teach."

Roger looked at Rob and half-smiled.

Roger Choiu: Yeah, she sent three of those guys down to see me. I didn't really see it as a big deal. I told the boys to cool it and sent them back to class. You know—guys are guys.

Lynn: You are kidding, right? You can't really believe saying things like that is OK!

Roger: C'mon, Lynn. I'm not surprised you feel that way. You're a counselor. You're supposed to be overly sympathetic and touchy feely. I'm in charge of discipline, and I don't have time to deal with trivial things like name-calling.

Tom: Whoa here. Back up a minute. Let's not get into an argument over roles. We all have our jobs. What do the rest of you think about this? Is it serious?

There were some surprised looks when John Coast, the school resource officer, spoke up. He never talked at these meetings, and most of them wondered why he even came unless a crime had been committed earlier.

John Coast: I think it's very serious, and I'm sure not a "touchy-feely" guy! I hear boys all the time call girls names, brush up against them, even touch them in places we would have expelled for when I was in school.

Roger: Come on, John! Don't you think those girls like it? Do you ever hear them complain?

Jan Hulstead: I hate to admit it, but Roger does have a point. Our sexual harassment policy says the behavior must be "unwelcome" to be considered sexual harassment.

Lynn: Just because the girls don't complain doesn't mean they "welcome" it! After all, obviously nothing happened to the boys when their teacher reported it.

Once more Mr. Raydon interceded.

Tom: Instead of pointing fingers, let's try to solve this problem, if it is a problem. Suggestions? Do you want me to talk to the offenders?

When Kyle Jordan, the social worker, spoke up, it was also a surprise. Most of the time he added little to the conversation at these meetings. He was only in the building two days a week and had little interaction with the other staff.

Kyle Jordan: With all due respect, sir, I think the problem may need more attention than that. I've read a lot on the subject of peer harassing and bullying, and it has a very detrimental effect on learning. Several kids, mostly ninth- and tenth-grade girls, have mentioned incidents to me, but didn't want anyone to know about them. (The ninth- and tenth-grade counselors both nodded.) Another thing that bothers me is how all the kids pick on the students they think are gay or lesbian. I've had to actually walk some of the girls halfway home so no one would hurt them.

Tom: (Looking thoughtful) Maybe this is a bigger problem than it looks like. It does seem to me though that we may be blowing it out of proportion.

Roger: I'll say! You're all taking a little harmless flirting and normal teen stuff and making a big deal out of it! As far as the gay kids are concerned, maybe they should keep their sexual preferences to themselves. It works for the military!

Lynn: (gaping) You must be kidding!

Tom: I don't want to spend any more time on this topic right now. Why don't you counselors get together and see if this is serious and bring some suggestion to our next meeting about what if anything needs to be done.

As the meeting broke up Roger was heard telling Rob Galleger: "Wonderful. All we need is for the counselors to tell us one more way to coddle the kids into being 'politically correct.'"

Discussion Questions

1. How could it be determined if the behavior of the boys was unwelcome?
2. Who else should be involved in these discussions?

Chapter 5

3. What can be done about attitudes of "It's only flirting"?
4. What should the principal have done during this discussion? Was his decision to put only counselors on the committee a wise one? Why or why not?
5. What would you have said if you had been in the meeting?
6. What should the counselors do next?
7. What is the best possible solution to the problem in Donna's class?
8. What needs to be done to address the issues brought up concerning harassment of LGBT students?
9. Is this a typical midsize high school?
10. What is the policy in your school? Does it work?

6

Internet Issues

Russell met Ben coming into school one morning. "Hey Ben, glad you're here early, Dude. Come to the computer lab with me. I wanna show you what I found on Derek's home page last night. It is so funny!"

"OK. Let me drop off my math paper first. Weird Wilson threatened to call my folks if I missed one more assignment."

When Ben walked into the computer lab Russell already had the site pulled up and was laughing hysterically. "Look at this! Derek is so bad! He put a picture of Sonya Carter's face on this babe that stars in porn flicks! And look at the caption: 'Who has the balls to go after this busty babe? Call her for some good down-under action at 555-1234.' That's her real phone number, Man! I can't wait to see how many guys call her! She is so snooty she thinks she's too good to go out with guys like us. This oughta fix her!"

"Yeah," Ben said. "That's pretty funny, all right. But what's gonna happen if a teacher finds out?"

No Child Left Behind requires students to be technology-literate upon completion of the eighth grade. Even if it were not required by law, schools that did not include technology in their curriculum would be doing a huge disservice to today's students. But that is not the case. According to the National School Boards Association, at least 96 percent of school districts report that their teachers assign tasks requiring Internet use. So students who harass or bully other students have a tool available to them today that most of their parents had not even heard of when they were in school—the Internet.

As recently as a few years ago children and teenagers only had access to e-mail. Now with the addition of instant messaging, blogging, and multiuse sites such as MySpace and Facebook, the possibilities for students harassing each other are limitless.

As they should be, parents and educators are extremely concerned about adults exploiting and molesting children and youth electronically. What is of less concern, simply because it is not as well publicized, is the number of incidents of students harassing *each other*— peer sexual harassment. The occurrences have gone far beyond the nuisance stage. Like other forms of peer sexual harassment, they cause students to become depressed or ill, or to turn to alcohol and drugs and drop out of school.

In the days of e-mail only, students could control whether or not they read harassing statements, and they were the only ones who had access to their e-mails, so their peers could not see the derogatory remarks that other students sent them. That changed when instant messaging and blogging came on the scene. Now if a student is harassed online, many other students witness the harassment.

INSTANT MESSAGING

MySpace, the most widely used site of its kind, has more than 100 million members. Many of them are middle or high school students. In fact, according to information provided from MySpace, 61 percent of teenagers have a personal profile on a social networking site, and 71 percent of those teens access the Internet from school. Some of the students who post on MySpace are much younger than teenage. Although MySpace has a policy stating that users must be at least fourteen years of age, it cannot possibly catch all of the underage students who utilize the website.

MySpace allows students to create their own profile pages, which can include photos of themselves and others as well as links to pages outside the MySpace environment. Unfortunately, students who would not consider being mean, cruel, or harassing to another student face-to-face do not hesitate to harass others in writing. Printed words can be just as devastating to the victim as words hurled at them in the hallways. Electronic messages can cause embarrassment, fear, and depression, just as verbal remarks and threats do.

MySpace claims to take cyberbullying issues seriously. Under the heading of cyberbullying would be, among other things, peer/peer sexual harassment. If a student is being harassed or bullied he/she should take the following steps:

1. Click "Contact MySpace" located on the bottom of any My-Space.com Web page.
2. Select "reporting abuse" from the first dropdown menu.
3. Select "cyberbullying" in the second dropdown menu.
4. Follow any and all subsequent directions.

When the report reaches MySpace, they investigate and take appropriate action. MySpace recommends that the user block the cyberbully (harasser) from contacting them and remove the account immediately. The user is instructed not to delete any of the messages until the matter is resolved. Those are indeed good steps to take, but that does not prevent the alleged harasser from continuing the harassment of the student by spreading rumors about her/him on other sites.

Let's face it; most teachers and administrators do not know nearly as much as their students know about navigating communication sites on the Internet. Many of them don't even understand the vocabulary. Willard (2005) uses the following words to describe seven types of cyberbullying:

- Flaming—Sending angry rude or vulgar messages directed at a person or persons privately or to an online group
- Harassment—Repeatedly sending a person offensive messages
- Cyberstalking—harassment that is highly intimidating or includes threats of harm
- Denigration (put-down)—Sending or posting harmful untrue or cruel statements about a person to others
- Masquerading—Pretending to be someone else and sending or posting material that makes that person look bad or places that person in danger
- Outing and trickery—Sending or posting material about a person that contains sensitive private or embarrassing information, including forwarding private messages

- Exclusion—Actions that specifically and intentionally exclude a person from an online group, such as exclusion from instant messaging buddies lists

All of these practices are negative. All of them are hurtful. All of them have the potential to hurt a child academically, to harm him or her socially and emotionally, and to prevent learning. In more serious situations use of the Internet to harass others can lead to depression and even suicide.

According to the federal government, school personnel who understand their obligations under Title IX are in the best position to prevent harassment and to lessen the harm to students. In addition to Title IX, there are other laws that govern schools in regard to the Internet. Two of these are the Children's Internet Protection Act (CIPA) and the Neighborhood Children's Internet Protection Act (NCIPA).

Both of these acts supply funding or discounts if the school follows certain requirements such as filtering or blocking software and putting Internet policies in place to protect minors. Schools are obligated to provide safe places for children. But just as schools cannot always prevent shooting rampages, neither can they guarantee that their best efforts will always result in protecting minors from peer harassment over the Internet.

Common sense tells us that students of all ages should be supervised when using a computer at school. But in reality, there are sometimes legitimate reasons that students may be in the computer lab without teacher supervision. Students are assigned research and sent to the computer lab, which may be unsupervised. Even if the computer being used for the research is in the classroom with a teacher present, it only takes a minute to check one's e-mail or blog and send a message to another student.

Unlike face-to-face harassment, electronic harassment is rarely observed by teachers and rarely reported to adults at the school. It can go on for months or even years and do immeasurable harm to students. Young people are very technology literate and can send messages anonymously. Even though a student may suspect who the harasser is, it is difficult to prove without a technology expert being involved.

FREE SPEECH AND ELECTRONIC SEXUAL HARASSMENT

So how can the school prevent electronic harassment, and is the school liable when it does occur? What if it happens at home? Is a school district violating a student's freedom of speech if he/she is punished for comments on a website? We have already established from *Davis v. Monroe* (1999) that if a school has knowledge of one student harassing another and takes no steps to address the violation, then the school district is indeed liable for the actions of the harasser.

As far as responsibility of the school for messages from a home computer, the courts have usually paid attention to where the information was accessed, not where it was created. A case involving a student who solicited funds to hire a hit man to kill a teacher was posted on a website created at home but was accessed by students at school. The justices said that where speech that is aimed at a specific school and/or its personnel is brought onto the school campus or accessed at school by its originator, the speech would be considered on-campus speech (*J.S. v. Bethlehem Area School District*, 2002). Therefore the school district would be liable for any sexual harassment incidents *if they had knowledge of the incidents.*

When threats or derogatory or harmful remarks are posted on sites and are being accessed from school computers, some school districts have contacted the Internet service provider and had the website shut down. In one such case from Indiana the school also suspended the student responsible for the harmful messages he had posted on the free website. With the backing of the ACLU the student sued the district, claiming his rights to free speech had been violated. The school district settled the case out of court.

If the district had just shut down access to the site from the school and had not suspended the student, would the result have been the same? If they had taken no action would they have been liable under Title IX and *Davis*? To answer those questions we need to look briefly at the three Supreme Court cases that deal directly with free speech.

Tinker v. Des Moines Independent Community School District

In *Tinker* (1969), the landmark case dealing with free speech for students, students wore black armbands to school to protest the U.S. involvement in the Vietnam War. The school banned the wearing of armbands, and when the students wearing the armbands were disciplined they sued the school district claiming violation of their First Amendment right to free speech. The Supreme Court held that wearing the armbands was expressive conduct protected by the First Amendment. The Court determined that the school did not have a

compelling interest to prevent the armbands. They coined the memo-
rable quote, "Students do not forfeit their rights at the schoolhouse
gate."

The two-prong test used by the *Tinker* court was (1) whether or not
the speech was protected under the First Amendment and (2) whether
or not the action caused actual or foreseeable disruption in the
school. The Court held that the speech was indeed protected and that
it did not cause a disruption of educational activities at the school.
Thus the school did not have a compelling interest to ban the message
conveyed by the armbands.

Immediately following the *Tinker* decision students began to say
things like "You can't tell me what I can and cannot say; I have a right
to free speech." Even though the *Tinker* Court did not condone obscene speech, the "schoolhouse gate" quote got so much attention that
I am convinced that it was that case, not the removal of prayer from
public schools, that caused the decline in respect for authority and led
to obscene speech in classrooms and hallways of public schools.

Bethel School District v. Fraser

Seventeen years after the *Tinker* case the U.S. Supreme Court once
again addressed the issue of First Amendment rights for students. In
Bethel (1986) a high school student, Fraser, was suspended for giving a
nominating speech for a fellow student that referred to the candidate
in terms of "elaborate, graphic, and explicit sexual metaphor." Fraser
brought suit against the school district claiming violation of his First
Amendment right to free speech. The Court recognized and reaffirmed
the *Tinker* holding concerning free speech, but indicated that student
expressive rights were not as extensive as those of adults. Speech that
intrudes upon the work of the school is not allowed. The Court made
clear that vulgar, indecent, or disruptive speech can be punished. The
justices noted that even Congress is not allowed to use profane speech.

Hazelwood School District v. Kuhlmeier

Two years later the nation's highest court heard the third case concerning free speech for public school students. *Hazelwood* (1988)
asked a slightly different question. In this case a principal removed articles from the school paper that concerned sexual activities of some
of the students, articles on children from divorced parents, and arti-

cles concerning birth control. The principal said he thought the articles were inappropriate for the younger readers and that the articles contained identifying information of some of the students who had been discussed in the articles.

The students sued the school, claiming violation of their First Amendment rights. The question in this case was whether or not the school had to tolerate certain types of speech and also whether the school was forced to actively promote (as in the school newspaper) student speech with which it disagreed. As in *Bethel*, the Court cited *Tinker*, but said that the standard in *Tinker* was not the appropriate standard to address the issue in *Hazelwood*.

> We conclude that the standard articulated in *Tinker* for determining when a school may punish student expression need not also be the standard for determining when a school may refuse to lend its name and resources to dissemination of student expression. . . . [E]ducators do not offend the First Amendment . . . so long as their actions are reasonably related to legitimate pedagogical concerns." (*Hazelwood*, 1988, p. 272)

Perhaps the quote that should please school personnel and others who are concerned about vulgarity in schools the most is this one taken from *Bethel*:

> Surely it is a highly appropriate function of public school education to prohibit the use of vulgar and offensive terms in public discourse. Indeed, the 'fundamental values necessary to the maintenance of a democratic political system' disfavor the use of terms highly offensive or highly threatening to others. Nothing in the Constitution prohibits the states from insisting that certain modes of expression are inappropriate and subject to sanction.

Looking at the above Supreme Court cases, we can see that even if speech is protected, the school can still regulate it. That applies to Internet cases, even though the Supreme Court has not heard a case involving Internet harassment. Some speech found on the Internet may be protected, but the school can restrict it if it can show the speech is likely to create a substantial disruption at school.

Recent Cases Dealing with Internet Use

We would be remiss if we didn't look at lower-court cases that have involved students being punished because of their speech over the Internet.

As noted above, the United States Supreme Court has yet to hear a case involving students claiming free speech violations via the Internet, but several lower courts have heard such cases. *Lovell by Lovell v. Poway Unified School District* (1994) a case out of the ninth circuit, *Doe v. Pulaski County Special School District* (2001) from the eighth circuit, *and J.S. v. Bethlehem Area School District #14* (2000), a case out of Pennsylvania, all concerned threats, and all were found to be unprotected speech by their respective appellate courts.

Cases involving peer sexual harassment, however, don't always or even often contain threats. Most embarrass, humiliate, and may intimidate other students, but don't necessarily threaten their lives. So what does that mean? Are school officials powerless? No. The victims are still covered by the guidelines under Title IX dealing with sexual harassment. In addition, of course, the holdings of *Tinker, Bethel,* and *Hazelwood* apply regarding free speech violations.

The other prong under *Tinker* was proving if the action was disruptive to the educational process. What if it just disrupted one student's life? Is that enough? Certainly being sexually harassed by another student causes disruption of the educational process of the victim. However, a student should not have to prove that the educational process was disrupted; only that the school policy on sexual harassment was disobeyed.

WHAT CAN BE DONE

So what then is the solution to sexual harassment that occurs electronically? First and most important, each school must have a written sexual harassment policy. It should be written in language the students can understand, and it should be explained to the students and then sent home for a parent signature. As is often the case, communication will go a long way toward preventing infractions of the rules.

Second, the school should have a policy regarding Internet usage. That policy also should be explained to the students and sent home for the parents to sign.

Third, it is the responsibility of the administration to be sure the faculty and staff understand the importance of supervision when students are accessing a computer at school. Faculty should be made aware that the problem goes beyond students "playing on the computer when they should be listening." It is a matter of safety and liability. Most important, it is a matter of protecting students from other students who can damage them emotionally and educationally.

While communicating and enforcing policy and closely supervising students will not entirely alleviate the problem of students harassing their peers electronically at school, it will go a long way toward stopping it. To stop the harassing that originates from home computers it is important that school officials warn students that anything accessed at school is under the jurisdiction of the school, and illegal activities will not be allowed.

One caution—administrators should not be overly anxious to discipline students for misusing electronics without thoroughly investigating the circumstances. A 1998 case out of Missouri was brought by a student who was suspended for content found on his Web page that had been created from his home computer (*Beussink v. Woodland*, 1998). His home page contained a hyperlink to the school website and lampooned school officials. He used vulgar language on the site. After a student showed the site to a teacher, the teacher showed it to the principal. The principal suspended the student for ten days because of the content of the page.

The district court held for the student, saying that schools may not punish students for content of personal home pages unless the material creates a substantial disruption. Unfortunately, though the material may have actually created a "substantial disruption," the administrator suspended the student so quickly that it was difficult to know what could have happened. The *Beussink* court said that just being upset by the content of a student's speech is not justification for limiting the speech and that the site did not create a substantial disruption. Similar holdings were found in *Beidler v. North Thurston* (2000) and *Emmett v. Kirkland* (2000).

The court was upholding the student's right to free speech, but the outcome would have been different if the school could have shown disruption. Citing *Tinker* the school could have disciplined the student and been within their rights. *Beussink* only made it to the district court, and perhaps would have turned out differently if appealed, but it is a good reminder that schools have to have a good reason to curtail student speech. Substantial disruption is such a reason.

Note however that if *Beussink* had been a case involving peer sexual harassment, disobeying the school policies on sexual harassment and electronic issues would probably have been enough to uphold the discipline when the site was accessed at school. For a case that did prove disruption, see *J.S. v. Bethlehem* (2002). All of the above cases concerned speech accessed at school, but none of these cases specifically concerned student-to-student sexual harassment.

Looking at the case history, it cannot be stressed enough that just like face-to-face peer sexual harassment, the best offense is a good defense.

- All school personnel must be diligent in monitoring student activities.
- Sexual harassment policies must be in place and students and staff must understand them.
- Electronic policies must be in place and students and staff must understand them.
- Policies should be sent to all parents and discussed with them whenever possible.

Schools should not live in fear of litigation. They should know the laws and inform their constituents of them. Certainly free speech rights of students should not be ignored. Students can be protected from peer sexual harassment without trampling on another student's right to free speech. Administrators need to be aware of what speech is protected. Not all speech is protected. All students should be. Someone should tell that to Russell from the scenario.

Sample Electronic Policies

The two policies below are meant to give administrators and other policy makers a guide for writing their own Internet use policy for their district. Both of the policies could be improved, especially the language if they are intended for students, but they will at least give the policy makers an idea of what needs to be included in an acceptable-use policy. The policies do not, of course, concentrate on peer sexual harassment, but that subject should be included in such a policy. It will not take the place of the district's sexual harassment policy.

Policy #1

The school's information technology resources, including e-mail and Internet access, are provided for educational purposes. Adherence to the following policy is necessary for continued access to the school's technological resources.

Students must:

1. Respect and protect the privacy of others.
   - Use only assigned accounts.
   - Not view, use, or copy passwords, data, or networks to which they are not authorized.
   - Not distribute private information about others or themselves.
2. Respect and protect the integrity, availability, and security of all electronic resources.
   - Observe all network security practices, as posted.
   - Report security risks or violations to a teacher or network administrator.
   - Not destroy or damage data, networks, or other resources that do not belong to them without clear permission of the owner.
   - Conserve, protect, and share these resources with other students and Internet users.
3. Respect and protect the intellectual property of others.
   - Not infringe copyrights (no making illegal copies of music, games, or movies!).
   - Not plagiarize.
4. Respect and practice the principles of community.
   - Communicate only in ways that are kind and respectful.
   - Report threatening or discomforting materials to a teacher.
   - Not intentionally access, transmit, copy, or create material that violates the school's code of conduct (such as messages that are pornographic, threatening, rude, discriminatory, or meant to harass).
   - Not intentionally access, transmit, copy, or create material that is illegal (such as obscenity, stolen materials, or illegal copies of copyrighted works).
   - Not use the resources to further other acts that are criminal or violate the school's code of conduct.
   - Not send spam, chain letters, or other mass unsolicited mailings.
   - Not buy, sell, advertise, or otherwise conduct business, unless approved as a school project.

Students may, if in accord with the policy above:

1. Design and post Web pages and other material from school resources.

2. Use direct communications such as IRC, online chat, or instant messaging with a teacher's permission.
3. Install or download software, if also in conformity with laws and licenses, and under the supervision of a teacher.
4. Use the resources for any educational purpose.

Violations of these rules may result in disciplinary action, including the loss of a student's privileges to use the school's information technology resources.

School and network administrators and their authorized employees monitor the use of information technology resources to help ensure that uses are secure and in conformity with this policy. Administrators reserve the right to examine, use, and disclose any data found on the school's information networks in order to further the health, safety, discipline, or security of any student or other person, or to protect property. They may also use this information in disciplinary actions, and will furnish evidence of crime to law enforcement.

The policy should close with a place for the parents' and student's signature acknowledging that they have read and understood it. Parents should also be encouraged to discuss the policy with their child and to seek further information at www.cybercrime.gov.

The above policy, however, is flawed in that it is not written in student-friendly language. For example, in the first paragraph instead of saying "Adherence to the following policy is necessary for continued access to the school's technology resources," why not say "Students (or You) must follow the rules if they (you) want to use the school's technology, including computers.

In addition, the three statements that apply to sexual harassment or misconduct are not specific enough. They are:

1. Students must not distribute private information about themselves or others.
2. Students must communicate only in ways that are kind or respectful
3. Students may not intentionally access, transmit, copy, or create material that violates the school's code of conduct (such as messages that are pornographic, threatening, rude or discriminatory, or meant to harass.)

The statements, particularly number 2, are not specific enough. The third statement is better, but it doesn't sound firm enough to make a typical student beware of the consequences. Peer sexual harassment is serious. We cannot afford to tiptoe around students in a policy. Either the policy should contain specific examples of messages that violate the code of conduct, or the student should be referred to the school's policy on sexual harassment.

Policy #2

The terms and conditions are:

1. Acceptable-use access to the district's Internet must be for the purpose of education or research and must be consistent with the educational objectives of the district.
2. The use of the district's Internet is a privilege; not a right, and inappropriate use will result in a cancellation of those privileges. The technology director, in conjunction with the appropriate building administrator, will make all decisions regarding whether or not a user has violated this policy and may deny, revoke, or suspend access at any time.
3. Unacceptable use: You are responsible for your actions and activities involving the network. Some examples of unacceptable uses are:
   a. Using the network for any illegal activity, including violation of copyright or other contracts or transmitting any material in violation of any U.S. or state regulation
   b. Downloading of software without authorization by the supervisor (teacher) regardless of whether it is copyrighted or scanned for viruses
   c. Downloading copyrighted materials for other than personal use
   d. Using the network for private financial or commercial gain
   e. Wastefully using resources, such as file space
   f. Gaining unauthorized access to resources or entities
   g. Invading the privacy of individuals
   h. Using another user's account or password
   i. Posting material authored or created by another without his/her consent

   j. Posting anonymous messages
   k. Using the network for commercial or private advertising
   l. Accessing, submitting, posting, publishing, or displaying any defamatory, inaccurate, abusive, obscene, profane, sexually oriented, threatening, ethnically offensive, harassing, or illegal material
   m. Using the network while access privileges are suspended or revoked
   n. Plagiarism of any type
4. Network Etiquette: You are expected to abide by the generally accepted rules of network etiquette. These include but are not limited to the following:
   a. Be polite. Do not become abusive in your messages to others.
   b. Use appropriate language. Do not swear or use vulgarities or any other inappropriate language.
   c. Do not reveal your full name, personal address, or telephone number, nor those of students or colleagues. (Use only your first name.)
   d. Recognize that electronic mail (e-mail) is not private. People who operate the system have access to all mail. Messages relating to or in support of illegal activities may be reported to the authorities.
   e. Do not use the network in any way that would disrupt its use by other users.
   f. Consider all communications and information accessible via the network to be private property.
   g. Include your name and school at the bottom of e-mail but never give your home address or phone number.
   h. Use all capitals only to highlight a word. If you use them for an entire message, people will think you're shouting.

The remainder of the policy discusses security issues, vandalism issues, credit card charges, viruses, inspection, and filters. An authorization that must be signed by the user and the parent is included.

Though better than the first policy, this one also has some faults. One major flaw is the language. For example, "Gaining unauthorized access to resources or entities" needs to be put into more age-appropriate language, as does "Consider all communications and information accessible via the network to be private property." Sentences like those won't mean a lot to a fifth grader.

In addition, the user is instructed to "Include your name and school at the bottom of the e-mail," while in earlier instructions he/she was told "Do not reveal your full name." It is almost human nature when told to include your name somewhere that you use your whole name.

When administrators and school board members sit down to write an acceptable-use policy, they need to look at several sample policies and take the best from each of them. The policies should be created to:

- Inform parents about the school's policies
- Explain to students the responsibilities that go along with electronic access
- Protect students from harmful and inappropriate material
- Encourage ethical behavior, polite communication, and individual integrity
- Protect the school equipment
- Simplify life for school IT personnel
- Discourage plagiarism and software piracy
- Inform users that online activities may be monitored by school personnel
- Reduce the risk of lawsuits

Well-written policies are a school district's best defense against misuse of electronics by students. That includes using computers to harass peers, but while most acceptable-use policies address computer use almost exclusively, there should also be policy concerning other electronic devices including cell phones.

The nation's largest school system, in New York City, has banned the use of cell phones and is now being sued because of the ban. Parents object to the ban, saying that they need to be in touch with their children. Detroit schools have also banned cell phones, as have many other districts.

While there may be some good uses of cell phones in schools (such as taking pictures of class projects) the negative far outweighs the positive. Students have been caught making drug deals on phones, sending test answers to other students, taking pictures of tests, and harassing other students by taking inappropriate pictures of them and sending them to other students.

When students do use cell phones inappropriately it is much more difficult to discover than it is to discover misuse of the Internet via computers. At the very least, students should turn off their phones at all times during school and never have them in plain sight.

The Internet is here to stay. Other electronic devices that the last generation did not have are also here to stay and becoming more advanced every day. It is sad when this great technology is used as one more way for students to sexually harass their peers. It is up to teachers, administrators, counselors, parents, and other responsible adults to educate and monitor children and teenagers as they utilize these new media.

Discussion Questions

1. What are some other ways not mentioned above that students can misuse electronic equipment?
2. How do those relate to harassing their peers?
3. Do you think cell phones should be banned from public schools? Why or why not?
4. What would you do if a student showed you an offensive message she/he had seen posted on the Internet and written by one of your students?

7

Legal Issues and Case History

SCENARIO

On a Friday afternoon, Roger Crampton, the principal of Liberty High School, hung up the phone and grimaced. That's all he needed this week—the threat of a lawsuit. In a district as big as this one lawsuits weren't uncommon, just always unwelcome. This one, if it transpired, sounded like it would be particularly messy. Roger didn't have any doubt, however, that the district would win it. Jake Bowser was threatening to sue the district, the superintendent, himself, and one of the choir teachers. It seems as though his tenth-grade daughter, Christy, was claiming she was being sexually harassed by some of the boys in her class.

"Oh, brother," Roger thought. "The guys were probably just flirting. Oh well, at least it wasn't a girl claiming to have been harassed by a teacher. Now that would really be messy. It is almost a sure bet that the school would not win one of those!"

Roger felt good that he annually talked with the staff about the seriousness of even a hint of impropriety. He had pounded it in: Never see a student in the gym alone one on one. Never shut the door to your classroom with a student after school. Never tell jokes in poor taste. Never touch a student. On and on. So far, the school had escaped any allegations brought by students against teachers.

This student/student thing, though, was just ridiculous. He was reminded of the suit brought several years ago when a six-year-old boy was suspended for kissing a six-year-old girl on the playground. The courts had thrown that one out. They would do the same with this if it ever got that far.

It was 5:20. Roger picked up his jacket and started for the door. He'd deal with this some other time. Right now he needed to get to the baseball game.

Three Weeks Later:

"Mr. Crampton, the superintendent is on line three."

"OK Kate. Put him on."

"Hi Ralph. What can I do for you?"

"Well, Roger, we may have something of a problem on our hands."

"What else is new?" Roger laughed.

"I'm afraid this may become serious if we don't nip it in the bud. An irate parent just called me about his daughter being picked on in her music class. Jake Bowser. He said he had spoken with you a couple of weeks ago, and you had assured him you would deal with the situation. What happened?"

Roger frowned. Oh yeah—the guy who claimed his daughter was having trouble with some of the guys in her choir class. He had meant to talk to Sandra Treel, the choir teacher. It had just slipped his mind.

"Gosh, Ralph, I guess I just dropped the ball. No problem. I'll talk to the teacher tomorrow. If we need to we'll transfer the girl out of the class."

"I'm afraid it's gone too far for that. Bowser is saying that his daughter had talked repeatedly with the teacher and even one of the counselors and nothing was done about the situation. He is going to see an attorney this afternoon. He mentioned Title IX and the Office of Civil Rights. It sounds like he's done his research."

"Good grief, Ralph. You can't be serious! He probably just Googled 'sexual harassment' and found an advocacy group that tells parents to sue for any reason. Besides, I know that Bowser girl—Christy—She's one of our cheerleaders and loose as a goose. She probably loves every minute of the attention! Isn't there something about actions must be 'unwelcome'? Trust me, I bet she invited whatever remarks the boys are making."

"Actually, according to her dad, there is more to it than just remarks. He said four times the boys had actually touched her inappropriately and once pushed her up against a cabinet. That in addition to calling her vulgar names."

"If it's that bad, then I guess I should have paid more attention. But honestly, students call each other names like 'slut' and 'whore' all the time these days. I hear it in the halls all the time. I'm telling you, Ralph, that girl is not exactly Miss Virginity. I bet she loves that attention."

The superintendent interrupted. "Be that as it may, you did drop the ball, Roger. Now we have a situation on our hands. I need you to be down here at my office first thing tomorrow morning. We'll meet with our attorney and see what we can do about this." With that, he hung up.

Roger Crampton shook his head in disgust. *"What a waste of time. The girl is a wild child. As soon is that is clarified, this will all go away."*

LEGAL HISTORY OF PEER/PEER SEXUAL HARASSMENT

While it is unfortunate that schools had to be sued before they began to do anything about peer sexual harassment issues, it is nevertheless a fact. Perhaps there were too many Roger Cramptons sitting in decision-making chairs.

Title IX of the Education Amendments of 1972 had been in place for two decades before it was cited in the Supreme Court case of *Franklin v. Gwinnett County Public Schools* (1992). Prior to that time sexual harassment suits *in the workplace* had been brought under Title VII of the Civil Rights Act of 1964. Though the circumstances were different in schools than in the workplace, those cases set the stage for challenging peer sexual harassment in the school. (See, for example, *Meritor Savings Bank v. Vinson* 1986.) Title VII has been used as a guidance for sexual harassment cases in the schools also. More recently, however, Title IX is the law utilized when dealing with school sexual harassment issues.

Legally, sexual harassment is considered a form of sex discrimination. Title IX provides that "No person in the United States shall, on the basis of sex, be excluded from participation in, be denied the benefits of, or be subjected to discrimination under any education program or activity receiving Federal financial aid to those educational institutions responsible for sexually discriminatory practices" (20 U.S.C. §1681 (a)).

First Major Case Utilizing Title IX

In *Franklin v. Gwinnett County Public Schools* (1992) the Court held that students could sue their schools for violations of Title IX and possibly obtain money damages. That case did not involve peer/peer sexual harassment, which we are examining here; instead it involved a high school student who alleged that she had been sexually assaulted and harassed by her *teacher*. According to the student, the school was aware of the harassment but took no action to stop it. Furthermore the student stated that the school discouraged her from pressing charges. The school had dropped the investigation in exchange for the teacher's resignation. The student claimed she had been subjected to sex discrimination and was entitled to monetary recovery under Title IX.

In a unanimous decision the Supreme Court agreed with the student, stating that Title IX places on public schools a duty not to discriminate on the basis of sex. The reasoning of the Court was that Congress would not have intended federal money to be spent to support the intentional discriminatory actions that they (Congress) had sought to eliminate with the passage of Title IX. The student was entitled to recover money under Title IX for the district's intentional discrimination, which was demonstrated by the school district's failure to stop the teacher's known sexual harassment of the student.

Cases concerning students harassing students began citing *Franklin*. The cases also cited Title IX, arguing that when student harass other students it creates a hostile environment. School officials who fail to stop the harassment should be held liable for the creation of a hostile environment.

The second part of the lawsuit is based on 42 U.S.C. § 1983, a civil rights statute that awards monetary damages in cases of constitution violations. The argument under that law is that students have a constitutional liberty interest in being free from abusive behavior, and that schools have a duty to maintain a safe environment for students.

Between 1995 and 1998 six federal appellate circuits issued rulings in peer sexual harassment cases. Four of the appellate circuits (covering twenty-three states) held that students could use Title IX to hold schools accountable for peer sexual harassment. Two other appellate courts covering six states ruled in the opposite way.

Then in 1999, to settle the issue of whether or not schools could be held liable for monetary damages for students who had been sexually harassed by their peers, the Supreme Court decided to hear the case of *Davis v. Monroe County Board of Education* (1999), which came out of the eleventh circuit.

The eleventh circuit court had ruled that the harm to LaShonda Davis had occurred because the school officials who knew about the harassment had failed to take action to stop the harassing. They stated that when an educational institution knowingly fails to take action to remedy a hostile environment caused by a student's sexual harassment of another student, the harassed student has been denied the benefits of or been subject to discrimination under that educational program in violation of Title IX.

The Davis Case at the Supreme Court Level

The case was decided by the Supreme Court of the United States in 1999, with the justices holding that school districts may be held liable only "where they are deliberately indifferent to sexual harassment, of which they have actual knowledge, that is so severe, pervasive, and objectively offensive that it can be said to deprive the victims of access to the educational opportunities or benefits provided by the schools" (*Davis v. Monroe County Board of Education*, 1999, p. 13).

Furthermore, Justice O'Connor, in writing the decision, stated:

> The common law also put schools on notice that they may be held responsible under state law for failing to protect students from third parties' tortuous acts. Of course the harasser's identity is not irrelevant. . . . If a recipient [of federal funds, i.e., the school] does not engage in the harassment directly, it may not be liable for damages unless its deliberate indifference subjects its students to harassment, i.e., at a minimum causes students to undergo harassment or makes them liable or vulnerable to it. . . . [T]he harassment must take place in a context subject to the school district's control. (*Davis v. Monroe County Board of Education*, 1999, p. 13)

Mr. Crampton and his district are in trouble!

Facts of Davis v. Monroe

Certainly the action of the student against Davis was severe, pervasive, and offensive. LaShonda Davis was a fifth-grade student who was harassed over a six-month period by a male fifth-grade student. The boy attempted to fondle her, attempted to touch her breasts and vaginal area, rubbed against her in a sexually suggestive manner, and made explicit sexual remarks. After each incident LaShonda told the teachers and her mother. LaShonda's mother repeatedly called the teacher and the principal. The school officials never removed or disciplined the boy in any way. The teacher continually denied LaShonda's request that her seat be moved away from the harasser, which was right next to hers. Talk about a travesty!

LaShonda claimed that her grades suffered, she lost the ability to concentrate on her homework, and her emotional and mental health declined. At one point she wrote a suicide note.

When the Eleventh Circuit Court of Appeals ruled in LaShonda's favor, the justices explained the elements that an alleged victim must prove to succeed in a peer sexual harassment case:

1. That she is a member of a protected group
2. That she was subjected to unwelcome sexual harassment
3. That the harassment was based on sex
4. That the harassment was sufficiently severe or pervasive so as to alter the conditions of her education and create an abusive educational environment
5. That some basis for institutional liability has been established (*Davis v. Monroe County Board of Education* 1996, p. 1194).

In ruling for LaShonda Davis, the Supreme Court recognized that students often engage in insults, banter, teasing, shoving, pushing, and other gender-related conduct that is upsetting to the students who are on the receiving end of these behaviors. Damages are not available for those simple acts. Instead, when addressing harassment between peers (student/student) the behavior must be so severe, pervasive, and objectively offensive that the victim is denied equal access to education protected by Title IX. The actions against LaShonda fell into that category.

The *Davis* Court recognized that the school officials have flexibility in decision making. All that is necessary for school officials to do is to respond to peer sexual harassment in a manner that is not unreasonable. Not responding to LaShonda's mother's pleas, or not even moving LaShonda away from her harasser, was clearly unreasonable. Mr. Crampton, by not responding to the complaints from Christy Bowser, makes his district liable for monetary damages based on *Davis* and the OCR Guidelines.

So the bottom line for school administrators to know is that the school can be held liable if a student is being sexually harassed by a peer and the school has knowledge of the incident(s).

RESPONSIBILITIES OF THE SCHOOL DISTRICT

The U.S. Department of Education's Office of Civil Rights (2001) detailed the responsibility of a school district regarding sexual harassment issues. The forty-page policy guide is entitled *Sexual Harassment Policy Guidance: Harassment of Students by School Employees, Other Students, or Third Parties.* According to the OCR procedural requirements, each district must designate a Title IX coordinator who is the one responsible for Title IX compliance (OCR, n.d.a.). Ideally, this person may be the employee designated to handle Section 504 complaints. The district must notify all its students and employees of the name, office, address, and telephone number of the Title IX coordinator. The coordinator is responsible for coordinating investigations into complaints and implementing regulations.

The person designated as Title IX coordinator should have an in-depth knowledge of the Title IX regulations as well as general knowledge of federal and state nondiscrimination laws. He/she should be well informed of the district's grievance procedures and be able to prepare reports and to communicate effectively. The administrator who designates the coordinator should not do so lightly. The coordinator must have the tact and skills necessary to mediate differences of opinion and to work with parents, students, and educators while maintaining a positive climate in what may be a hostile situation. He/she should be at the forefront of educating staff and students.

The OCR requires that the school district publish either in the newspaper or as a written communication to each student and school district employee notification of the district's Title IX policy. However, for a district to take the easy way out and only publish the notice in the newspaper is not a good idea. How many people actually read the legal notices in a newspaper? The answer, unfortunately, is a very small percentage of the public and in most cases *none* of the students. A responsible coordinator or administrator will make sure that all parties—parents, students, and school employees—have a copy of the notice and that they understand it. That means someone needs to go over the information with all involved.

This book is not the place to go into in-depth legal requirements for school districts. All pertinent information may easily be obtained through the Office of Civil Rights website. However, it is appropriate to mention four items here:

1. Title IX does not ban flirtation. Sexual overtures from student to student are not sexual harassment if the actions are welcome.
2. Trivial incidents of objectionable behavior are not sexual harassment. The incidents should be addressed, but counseling the

students involved and communicating with the parents is probably all that is required in many cases unless a complaint is filed. The objective of the district should be to stop all objectionable behavior while fitting the "punishment to the crime." Real incidents of sexual harassment should be addressed promptly; issues that do not fall under the definition of sexual harassment should be handled without blowing the incidents out of proportion.

3. Title IX does not suppress academic discourse, even if it is offensive. While teachers should be concerned if discussions inappropriate for the age of their students are going on in the classroom, those discussions are not against the law under Title IX.

4. Behavior covered by sexual harassment includes rape. Rape is a criminal activity, and the student should always press charges against the harasser and file a complaint with school officials.

Title IX does not require schools to adopt policies specifically prohibiting sexual harassment. It does require that they have procedures to address sex discrimination. The guidance published by the Office for Civil Rights (OCR, 2001) makes clear that having a policy and grievance procedures in place for dealing with sexual harassment issues will take away much of school districts' legal liability risk.

CONCLUSION

Schools must address sexual harassment. The law governing sexual harassment, Title IX, addresses sex discrimination. The Office of Civil Rights has issued specific guidelines for dealing with sexual harassment issues in public schools. Failure to comply with the regulations could result in loss of funding for the school district. Case law pertaining to peer sexual harassment comes from *Davis v. Monroe* (1999), which declared school districts could be liable for monetary damages if they had knowledge of the sexual harassment and did nothing to stop it. School districts must have sex discrimination policies and should specifically address sexual harassment within those policies or as a separate document.

Discussion Questions

Look again at the scenario at the beginning of the chapter and answer the following questions:

1. Who was responsible for letting the situation get out of hand?
2. What steps should have been taken before the situation escalated?
3. What should be done now?
4. Do you think the school district can stop this lawsuit? How?

8

Policy Development

SCENARIO

The seven board members and the superintendent of the Skyler School District, with 8,200 students, K–12 are having a mid-month meeting, called by the board president and not open to the public.

Ben Marston, president of the Board of Education for Skyler School District, called the meeting to order.

Ben Marston: *OK, people, as I told you in the letter, this is not a formal board meeting, but a policy meeting. That's why all of the public's chairs are empty and it's just us tonight. Before the policy is adopted, of course, we'll have open meetings and opportunities for the public to speak on what we've written. Ralph [the school district superintendent], is going to tell you what we're required to do when writing this policy.*

Kevin Barton: *What exactly is this policy about? It seems like we've written a policy for everything under the sun already. Are we going to start writing policy telling parents what they can complain about? Now that would be one I could approve of! Maybe I'd get fewer midnight phone calls!*

Chuckles from the other board members. "Hear Hear!"

Ben: *You're a dreamer, Kevin. No, this is a policy we need to write concerning sexual harassment of students by other students.*

Josie Telligrini: *We already have a sexual harassment policy in place. It's within the nondiscrimination policy. If I remember correctly, that wasn't an option. It's the law.*

Ben: *You're right, we do, Josie. But Ralph thinks this is necessary, so let's listen to what he has to say.*

Ralph Goldstein (superintendent): *Thanks, Ben. You're right. We've had a policy in place for several years now to cover discrimination issues, ever since the law required us to address Title IX issues. But recent research has shown that sexual harassment between and among students, in other words, peer sexual harassment, has not decreased and is a very serious problem. It leads to emotional distress, dropouts, physical harm, and even suicides among students.*

Josie: *Ralph, are you talking about harassment of gay and lesbian students?*

Ralph: *They are included, but that's just part of the problem. The most comprehensive study shows that as many as 80 percent of students in middle schools claimed to have been sexually harassed.*

Heather Brown: *You know ten years ago I would have said that was an exaggeration. But since my own kids have gone through middle school and I've been involved as a volunteer at Lincoln Middle School, that number doesn't surprise me at all. No one seems to pay any attention to the policy that is in place now.*

Ralph: *According to the information I received at the National Superintendents' Conference last week, that is the problem. All districts have the nondiscrimination policy in place, but no one pays any attention to the sexual harassment part unless they're involved in a suit involving an employee and a student. We all know how ugly that can be. However, student/student harassment is really hurting kids.*

Heather: *So what do we need to do? Tweak the policy?*

Ralph: *I wish it were that simple. I'm afraid what we really need to do is write a completely separate policy.*

Groans.

Ralph: *I know, I know. We've had some marathon sessions writing policy. But I've had my assistant researching, and she has copied off ten sample policies for us to look at. It might be tempting just to insert our district's name into the blank spots on the sample policies, but we were warned against doing that at the last administrators' conference. The policy needs to be written by us and for us. That doesn't mean that these handouts won't save us hours. I think they will.*

Richard Smeltz: *Wait. Stop. Back up. I'm not willing to commit hours of my time to this unless it is really necessary. Why can't we just add some paragraphs* to the nondiscrimination policy we already have? Maybe that isn't even necessary.

Ralph: *I hear what you're saying Dick. But obviously what we have isn't working now, so why would making a few changes fix it? This really is a serious problem.*

Josie: *Here's a thought: Maybe the policy is OK as it stands, and what we really need to do is make sure the students know about it. Maybe we just need to write some directives for the principals concerning how they get the information out to the staff and students.*

Ralph: *Your point is well taken, Josie, about the students not understanding the policy. Heck, they don't even know we have a policy. But even if we read it aloud to each of them, the way it reads now, they wouldn't understand it, and they don't even know how to define sexual harassment. We have to tell them the difference between harmless flirting and unwelcome sexual words and actions.*

Richard: *So what you're saying is that we can't get out of this. Do we need to have Jack Rogers here?*

Ralph: *Yeah, eventually. As our attorney, he will have to examine what we write for errors. Since that's his job—to keep us out of trouble—and since he is on retainer, we could have him at every session, but we seem to move faster when we write and then have him examine it later and make changes where necessary.*

Heather: *I agree. He tends to pontificate. So, let's get started. I say we each take one of the sample policies and underline what we can use to make our own.*

POLICY

Having a comprehensive, easily understood policy in place will not prevent all peer sexual harassment. Neither will just informing the students and staff of the consequences of sexual harassment prevent it from occurring. Only when a school climate is changed from one of fear and humiliation for some students to a campus where safety can be taken for granted and sexual harassment among students is not tolerated will peer sexual harassment be lessened. However, *not* having a good sexual harassment policy in place that is understood by students and staff is a sure recipe for the continuance of peer sexual harassment.

Not having a policy that addresses peer sexual harassment in the school should not be an option. All schools (or districts) should have a policy for the students as well as a separate policy for the staff and faculty. The staff and faculty must be educated on the policy that is distributed to the students.

The law requires that all school districts have a *nondiscrimination* policy in place. The OCR recommends that each school have a specific sexual harassment policy in place. Some states require all school districts to have a specific policy against sexual harassment in place. Other states include the sexual harassment policy within a broader policy against sexual discrimination. Having a separate policy (in addition to the policy that addresses quid pro quo sexual harassment) that addresses *only* student/student sexual harassment sends a stronger message to students that it will not be tolerated.

Taking the time to develop a policy that students can understand and then taking the time to explain it in detail to both the students and school personnel is time well spent. When students and staff recognize that the school board and administrators are so concerned with the problem of student/student sexual harassment that they are willing to spend time on it, they are more apt to realize that this is serious business: Student/student harassment will not be tolerated. Whichever method is selected, *every* school district should have a policy addressing sexual harassment. Having a school or district policy sends the message to the community that peer sexual harassment is taken seriously. For those who argue that class time is too valuable to spend time on this issue, inform them of the serious consequences to learning when students feel unsafe, uncomfortable, or humiliated. The gain in learning time in the long run will be significant!

Deliberations by the school board that will take place when the policy is being written or adopted are often the first time that the board members are aware of the scope of the problem. Because they are directly involved in writing and adopting the policy, the board members will be in a better position to examine the issues and to prevent litigation. But more importantly than that, the board members will become aware of the harm that is being done to students who are sexually harassed. They will be able to put their stamp of approval on a no-tolerance policy and in so doing they will improve the school climate, promote learning for all students, and prevent emotional harm to students.

There are numerous sample policies available for school districts to examine when writing their own policy. Most of these are available on the Internet. Some of those, supplied by the government office of the Office For Civil Rights, are available for download. They were published under the title *Protecting Students from Harassment and Hate Crimes: A Guide for Schools* (OCR, 1999).

This is important: A well-written policy to be read by school personnel is not necessarily the best policy to be distributed to the students. The policy or information in the handbook for students and parents *must* be in clear language that they can easily understand! In other words, students need their own edition of the policy. The opening paragraph needs to grab the attention of the students and parents, and they must be able to easily follow the guidelines. It should be in age-appropriate language, not "legalese." This user-friendly policy will contain much of the same information that the official policy does.

Whether school district officials elect to write their own official policy or use one of the sample policies as a template, the policy makers should discuss the policy line by line.

Elements of a Peer Sexual Harassment Policy

Set out below are the minimum elements that should be covered in a sexual harassment policy, with examples for each element. Policy makers will want to elaborate on these statements as appropriate for their district.

Statement of Commitment to Eliminating Peer Sexual Harassment

Example:

The _____ School District recognizes that in order for learning to take place, all students must learn in an environment free from sexual harassment between and among students. It is the policy and practice of the _____ School District to promote and maintain a safe learning environment for all students. The policy includes activities taking place while at school as well as at extracurricular activities under the supervision of _____ School District. Recognizing that peer sexual harassment results in an unsafe school climate, lower academic achievement, and social, emotional, and physical harm to students, any such harassment will not be tolerated.

A copy of this policy will be available to every student and all school personnel of _____ District. Violation of this policy by students or school personnel will result in prompt action following the guidelines contained within the policy.

Definition of Peer Sexual Harassment

Example:

The _____ District defines sexual harassment as follows:

Unwelcome verbal or physical sexual advances between and among students that cause the recipient or observer of the advances to be uncomfortable or cause distress of any kind.

Unwelcome sexual conduct that is so severe, persistent, or pervasive that it affects a student's ability to benefit from or participate in an educational program or activity, or creates a hostile environment for students.

Examples of conduct that may be considered sexual harassment include but are not limited to:
- Direct or indirect threats or bribes for unwanted sexual activity
- Sexual innuendos and comments
- Intrusive sexually explicit questions
- Sexually suggestive sounds or gestures such as sucking noises, winks, or pelvic thrusts
- Repeatedly asking a person out for dates or to have sex
- Touching, patting, pinching, stroking, squeezing, tickling, or brushing against a person
- A neck/shoulder massage
- Rating a person's sexual attractiveness
- Ogling or leering, staring at a woman's breasts or a man's derriere
- Spreading rumors about a person's sexuality
- Graffiti about a person's sexuality
- Name-calling such as "bitch," "whore," or "slut"
- Sexual ridicule
- Frequent jokes about sex
- Letters, notes, telephone calls, or material of a sexual nature
- Pervasive displays of picture calendars, cartoons, or other materials with sexually explicit graphic content
- Stalking a person
- Attempted or actual sexual assault according to OCR guidelines

Other definitions include:
- Sexual graffiti or messages on bathroom walls

- Derogatory terms such as "fag" or "lezzie"
- Spying on students dressing or showering at school
- Flashing or mooning
- Pulling clothing down or off
- Spiking (pulling down someone's pants) or "snuggies" (when underwear is pulled up at the waist)

(Note to policy writers: While listing the examples may appear to take up a lot of room in the policy, it is very important that students be given specific examples that can be considered sexual harassment.)

Reporting Procedures

Example:

Any student who believes she/he has been the victim of peer sexual harassment should report the alleged harassment to the appropriate school personnel immediately. Students should report the incident to (1) any teacher, (2) any counselor, (3) the principal, or (4) the school compliance officer. Students are encouraged to verbally report the incident(s) to one of the above people immediately to seek assistance for formally reporting the incident. The school staff member who hears the report will assist the student in taking the next step in the reporting procedure.

Nothing in this policy shall prevent the student(s) from reporting the incident directly to the superintendent of schools or the compliance officer. Any person with knowledge or belief that a student has or may have been the victim of peer sexual harassment must immediately report the incident(s) to the appropriate school official.

If a student reports the incident to a school employee other than the school compliance officer, that person should, upon receipt of the report, without screening or modifying it in any way, report the incident(s) to the district compliance officer. The district compliance officer for _____ District is _____.

The district compliance officer shall:

1. Oversee the investigative process
2. Ensure that an impartial investigator who has been trained in the procedures and standards necessary to identify unlawful harassment conducts the investigation
3. Recommend appropriate discipline and remedies when necessary
4. Take any appropriate action to rectify the damages caused by the harassment, including protection of the victim during the investigation

A charge of peer sexual harassment may also be investigated by the Office for Civil Rights of the U.S. Department of Education, which may be contacted at the Office for Civil Rights, U.S. Department of Education, Region _____ [address of regional OCR office] _____.

A student who has been harassed may file a lawsuit under a state statute or under Title IX of the federal Civil Rights Act of 1964. The student or guardian should consult with a private attorney about these options.

Investigation

Example:

Upon receiving a complaint of peer sexual harassment, the district compliance officer shall immediately undertake an investigation of the complaint. The investigation may be conducted by school district officials or by a third party designated by the district.

The investigation may include personal interviews with involved parties or with parties who have information relevant to the alleged incident(s). The investigation may also include examination of any written documents.

In determining whether or not the incident(s) violate this policy, the investigator may consider:

- The nature of the behavior—severity
- The persistence of the behavior
- The intrusiveness of the behavior
- The unwelcomeness factor
- The relationship between the parties involved
- The age and sex of the victim
- The age and sex of the alleged harasser
- Whether the alleged harasser(s) have been involved in previous incidents
- Whether the conduct adversely affects the student's education or created a hostile environment

The investigation shall take place no later than _____ days following the written receipt of the complaint.

The investigation shall result in a report, which will be filed with the office of the superintendent. If the superintendent has been named in the complaint, the report shall go directly to the school board.

This investigation shall be conducted regardless of whether or not a criminal investigation of the matter is pending or has been concluded.

Action Resulting from an Investigation

Example:

The school district will take prompt action, which may include, but is not limited to:

- Counseling of both the alleged harasser and the alleged victim
- Awareness training
- Parent conferences
- Detention
- Warning
- Suspension from school
- Suspension from selected activities
- Expulsion
- Transfer
- Other disciplinary actions practiced by _____ School District.

Copies of all complaints shall be maintained in the superintendent's office.

Reprisal

Example:

Reporting of an alleged incident of sexual harassment shall in no way affect the complainant's grades, learning, or school environment. The school district will discipline any student or school staff member who retaliates against a complainant or informer. Retaliation includes any form of intimidation, reprisal, or harassment.

Publication of Policy Procedures

Example:

A copy of this policy shall be posted in each school.
A copy of this policy shall be posted on the school district website.
A copy of this policy with specific rules for school personnel will be published in the Teacher/Employee Handbook.
A notice will be sent home to every parent announcing where the policy may be accessed.
The student portion of this policy will be included in the student handbook, which is sent home with every student. Parents or guardians will be required to sign the policy acknowledging they have read it.

The policy shall be reviewed each year for compliance with federal and state laws and district and school regulations.

CONCLUSION

Numerous school districts recognize the value of a sexual harassment policy, and many address student/student sexual harassment issues. We must however go beyond that. Districts need to have a separate policy for students that they can understand. Each school should make sure that every student has read the policy or that it has been read to them. Whatever it takes to educate students about what constitutes sexual harassment and what will happen when it occurs must be done. Spending time every year on the issue will result in better understanding, fewer incidents of sexual harassment, and increased learning.

Not having a policy that students can understand should never be an option.

Discussion Questions

1. Who should be responsible for writing the sexual harassment policy?
2. Who should be responsible for providing input? What constituencies?
3. How should the policy changes be published?
4. Should the faculty be allowed to vote on the policy?
5. Should students be allowed to offer input?
6. What legal considerations are important when writing policy?
7. If you were in charge of writing the policy, what would be your first step?

9

What Can Parents and Students Do?

SCENARIO

Marsha pulled up in the driveway just as her seventeen-year-old daughter, Melanie, got out of her friend's car. The friend drove off, and Melanie walked dejectedly into the house.

"Hey, Mel," Marsha called, "How was school?"

"OK."

"C'mon, girl. Talk to me. You've been saying 'OK' for two weeks now. What's going on? Are you tired?"

"I'm fine, Mom. I gotta go study."

Marsha frowned as she watched her daughter go up the stairs. What was going on with her confident, outgoing daughter? She didn't even act this sullen when she was thirteen. Wasn't junior year supposed to be a fun year?

Later that evening Marsha mentioned her concerns about Melanie's behavior to her husband.

"What do you think is going on, Trent? Neither of her sisters went through anything like this at this age. Is it just a stage? Is she taking too many AP classes? She has skipped volleyball practice twice lately, claiming she doesn't feel well. One more time and she'll be off the team."

"Honey," Mel's dad said, "girl problems are your domain. I did hear her say to Tasha on the phone the other day that she was really getting sick of the name-calling and that she was thinking of transferring into another history class. When I asked her about it she just said it was nothing."

"That doesn't really mean 'nothing,' Trent. It means she doesn't want to talk about it. I'll talk to her this evening."

Later when Marsha went into her daughter's room she found her staring at her computer screen. She didn't look like she was actually seeing it.

"Hey Mel, talk to me. Are you OK?"

"Sure, Mom. I'm fine."

"Sorry. That's not good enough," Marsha said as she sat down on the bed. "I want to know what's going on. Your dad said he heard you say you were thinking of transferring out of a class. Is that what you've been preoccupied with the past two weeks?"

Melanie didn't respond.

"C'mon, Honey. This is me. You can tell me what's bothering you."

"Oh, Mom, it's really nothing. Just some dumb kids who have started calling me names and, and stuff."

"What names? What 'stuff'?"

"Well if you must know, names like 'dyke' and 'butch.' Twice one of the guys in my history class actually squeezed my boob and said, 'So with a body like yours, you must be the girl in the relationships, right?'"

"What!" Marsha jumped up and walked over to Melanie. "Why didn't you tell us, Sweetheart? No one has the right to treat you like that! I'll have your dad call the school tomorrow morning. Better yet—he can take you to school and go in and talk with the principal in person! How did this all get started, anyway?"

"Oh, Mom, that's exactly why I didn't tell you. I knew you would react like this. Reporting this will only make it worse. And it's not just me. I'm not gay, anyway. It's just that all of a sudden someone heard that our volleyball coach is a lesbian, and now every girl on the team is being harassed like this. It's no big deal. I'm sure it will go away. It's just that now no boy will ever ask me out again, and I have another whole year at this school."

"Melanie," Marsha said quietly, "I know we let you fight your own battles, but not this time. Name-calling is bad, but touching you inappropriately is definitely sexual harassment, and your dad and I will not put up with it!"

"Mom, please! Let me handle it! You will only make it worse!"

"Sorry, Mel. Not this time. What other girls are being treated this way?"

What should students do if they think they have been sexually harassed? How can they determine if they actually are being harassed? What should students do who have witnessed a harassing incident? Who can help them?

The following feelings could alert a student that he/she is indeed being sexually harassed: confusion, guilt, helplessness, anger, hopelessness, fear, and a feeling of being alone. If students do experience sexual harassment, not always but in many cases the best scenario is for them to talk with their parents. A student and parent approaching the school with the problem carries a lot more weight than does a student alone. Officials are much less apt to take the attitude of "It's not serious" or "She (he) brought it on herself." Unfortunately, like Melanie, many students do not want the incident to be reported, for fear of a reprisal.

Students and parents have avenues of complaint and ways to address alleged sexual harassment incidents. The first thing they should do is contact a teacher or another staff person at the school. Many times students trust teachers more than other administrators or counselors because they know them better. Of course the student could always contact the principal or the compliance officer if she/he knew those people and felt comfortable talking to them about such a sensitive subject.

But what if the student does not want the parent involved? It takes a lot of nerve for a student to tell a school official about sexual harassment. Research has shown that only about 40 percent of students say they would be likely to report a sexual harassment incident between students to a school employee (AAUW, 2001, p. 14).

If the school has done a good job of informing the students and staff of the procedures, it will be easier for the student to complain even without a parent present. That, unfortunately, will not always be the case. If it were, students would be more inclined to report incidents and see the resolution without bringing their parents into it. That is not saying that parents should not have knowledge or be involved; it is just that many times things have gone on much longer than they should have by the time parents are aware of the situations.

A WORD TO STUDENTS WHEN PEER SEXUAL HARASSMENT IS SUSPECTED

The first thing you should do if you suspect that you have been sexually harassed by a peer is to let the alleged harasser know that the action is unwelcome at the time of the incident; you don't like it! If you are comfortable doing so, tell the person to stop, even though it may be embarrassing. Phrases like "Don't call me that. I don't like it," and "You're breaking the rules; harassment is against school policy" or "That was not funny; don't talk to me like that" or "You have no right to touch me" may be enough to stop the actions.

You should not be *forced* to confront your harasser. If you *do* feel like it would be safe to talk to the harasser, it is important to confront the person without his/her friends around if possible. If the student who is harassing you is confronted in front of his/her peers, he/she may be embarrassed and react by increasing the harassment. But once again, if you feel uncomfortable or unsafe confronting the alleged harasser alone, do not do so. Talk to an adult immediately.

Another thing to try is to avoid being around the harasser. This is easy to say, but if you have a class with the harasser, it will be almost impossible. But do not blame yourself. Being harassed is not your fault.

If the harassment persists, keep track of the incidents. Write them down with dates, times, places where they occurred, and a list of who witnessed the incidents. Save any notes or pictures you received from the harasser.

Tell an adult at the school whom you trust. If that person takes no actions, tell another adult. Find out who the compliance officer is (this should be in your school handbook) and tell that person what has been going on. Show the compliance officer the records you kept. This is not tattling. It is protecting yourself from abuse. If you are comfortable doing so, talk to your parents about what is going on at school. If you see another student being harassed, report that to a school official, and ask that your name be kept in confidence.

Note to school officials: It will often be expecting too much of a student to confront the harasser one on one if that is not comfortable for the victim, or if she or he fears retaliation. The job of the school is to provide a *safe* environment. Do not insist that the victim confront the student who is doing the harassing. The school is responsible for protecting the student, not for making them feel even more threatened.

ADVICE TO PARENTS

1. The first thing that you as a parent should do is talk to your children about sexual harassment, and encourage them to talk openly with you about harassment among or between students. It should

be stressed that harassment is not the same as flirting. Explain the difference between flirting and sexual harassment. Explain also that the action must be *unwelcome* to constitute harassment.

2. Read the school's sexual harassment policy, specifically the part regarding peer sexual harassment. Explain it to your child. Tell your child you will go with him/her to talk with school personnel.
3. Build the child's self-esteem.
4. Be an advocate for your child and other children you know who may be subjected to peer sexual harassment.
5. If you suspect your child or any other student has been or is being harassed, talk with her or him and then go to the school authorities—the teacher, principal, or compliance officer—immediately. Tell them the facts, and ask what they will do about the situation immediately.
6. If you have communicated with the school and the problem escalates instead of getting resolved, take your concerns to the district office. If you are still not satisfied, remember that you have a right to file a legal complaint with the U.S. Department of Education Office for Civil Rights and/or to bring litigation through the federal court system. Ask the compliance officer or the superintendent for a copy of the district's grievance procedure. Generally, complaints should be filed with the Office for Civil Rights within 180 days of the incident. The OCR investigation can be done independently of a lawsuit. The battle may be long and arduous, but children of any age are certainly worth the process.

Sexual harassment builds on stereotypes of females as the weaker sex and is about power more than sex. Parents who teach their children respect for the opposite sex and who actively seek ways to build their children's self-confidence will go a long way toward eliminating peer sexual harassment. If their children do encounter peer sexual harassment, they will be better equipped to handle it if their parents have communicated openly about issues of respect and the rights of all students to learn in a comfortable, safe environment.

CASE STUDY

Nicole is thirteen years old and an eighth grader at Mesa Middle School. For the past two months two boys in her homeroom class have been taunting her about the way she is built. This week they started suggesting that she meet them after school to explore what oral sex is all about.

At first Nicole ignored the boys, but then she started talking back to them, saying things like "F— off, Dickhead" and "Go screw yourself." Her math teacher, Ms. Jones, heard Nicole's comments, but not what the boys had said to Nicole. Consequently, Ms. Jones sent Nicole to the office, where she received a referral for using obscene language. When she got home her mom confronted her because the school had called her house to speak to a parent.

When Nicole explained to her mother that the boys had said "nasty things" to her first, her mom replied, "Too bad. They weren't the ones who got caught. You're grounded, young lady. Don't you ever talk like that again!"

The boys who had been bothering her thought the whole thing was hilarious. Their verbal taunts got worse, and during lunch hour they pushed her up against a locker and tried to kiss her. When Nicole's friend Alicia told her to tell a teacher, Nicole's reply was, "No way. Nobody would believe me. They think I'm a slut and a troublemaker."

Discussion Questions:

1. Who was at fault in this situation?
2. What should Nicole do now?
3. What do you think she *will* do? What will be the result?
4. What is the best thing that could happen for Nicole now?

10

A Final Word to Administrators

You should now have an overall view of the problem and how it should be handled by teachers, counselors, students, and parents. The problem will not go away, however, until school boards and administrators make it a priority to rid schools of peer sexual harassment. A systematic approach should be used to attack the causes: lack of respect for others, lack of respect for diversity and for the opposite sex, age-old attitudes that "kids will be kids," power plays, and attitudes based on ignorance. The problems will remain until attitudes change.

But solving those problems takes time. While they are being addressed, administrators must act immediately to prevent peer sexual harassment. School boards need to be aware of the seriousness of the problem and the effect it has on learning, not to mention the devastating effect it has on young lives. Administrators at the top need to be sure that the building administrators take charge and do more than post a statement saying the school has a sexual harassment policy.

All administrators are concerned about litigation, as well they should be. They should be aware that under the *Gebser v. Lago Vista Independent School Dist.* (1998) ruling and *Davis v. Monroe* (1999), their school district may be held liable for acts of sexual harassment under Title IX if (1) the plaintiff was subjected to gender-oriented conduct that was severe, pervasive, and/or persistent; (2) the sexual harassment denied the student an equal educational opportunity or benefit; (3) the district had "actual knowledge" of the sexual harassment; (4) the district was "deliberately indifferent" to the sexual harassment; and (5) the district's conduct caused the plaintiff damage.

Faculties need to passionate about alleviating the problem. Students need to be well informed and reassured that sexual harassment among students is no laughing matter and that it will be stopped. At the very least all incidents need to be investigated immediately, and students who report incidents of harassment need to be protected against retaliation from other students.

Adult supervision needs to be in place all over the school grounds. Every student needs to be aware that harassment will not be tolerated.

Practically speaking, principals should devote time to a plan based on the information presented in chapter 4. They should support the counselors and other school personnel who will be involved in presenting the plan to the faculty staff and students. They should set in place a program to educate the students on exactly what constitutes sexual harassment and what the consequences are. Parents should be given information that they can easily understand. Furthermore they should be assured that the teachers and administrators take peer sexual harassment very seriously. Parents should be included in discussions designed to lead to solutions to the problem of peer sexual harassment.

Peer sexual harassment has long-lasting effects. The self-esteem of a victim is always damaged. Serious harassment can lead to effects that may follow the student the remainder of her or his life. These results are well documented and usually obvious. What is less obvious and also very serious is the effect peer sexual harassment has on learning.

Over 20 percent of harassed students reported in the AAUW study said they did not want to go to school, and 24 percent said they did not talk as much in class as they did prior to being harassed. Sixteen percent found it hard to study (AAUW, 2001). Whether a student chooses to drop out of a class, drop out of school, or suffers from lowered grades and thwarted goals, it is a travesty. For educators to know about the problem and let it continue is a blight on our profession.

IF NOT YOU, THEN WHO?

It is a sad commentary on our profession that school officials did not do more to eliminate peer sexual harassment until the Supreme Court in *Davis v. Monroe* ruled that districts could be held liable if they knew about the harassment and took no actions to prevent it. Eventually the harasser in that case was charged with a felony. Administrators need to be aware that the law is the necessary tool to use in severe cases of harassment. That needs to be communicated to counselors and parents as well.

How can students learn to read, solve a mathematics equation, think critically about the causes of a war, or write a persuasive essay if they are being humiliated, intimidated, or threatened by her peers? They cannot. Schools *must* be safe places to be.

This must stop.

My comment to administrators and teachers is this: "If not you, then who?"

Discussion Questions

1. How can administrators find out how serious the problem of peer sexual harassment is in their school(s)?
2. How can administrators convince teachers that taking time to prevent peer sexual harassment is time well spent, when they already have so much to cover and so little time?
3. How can administrators utilize the input of *students* to solve this problem?
4. How could administrators determine if their preventive actions are working and worth the time spent?
5. Who should administrators consult before attacking the problem of peer sexual harassment?

References

AAUW (American Association of University Women). (2001). *Hostile hallways: the AAUW survey on sexual harassment in America's schools.* Available at: www.aauw.org (retrieved January 9, 2007)

ACA (American Counseling Association). (2005). *ACA Code of Ethics.* Section B. Available at: www.counseling.org/Resources/CodeOfEthics/TP/Home/CT2 .aspx.

Anderson, J., (2006). Sexual harassment letter from the editor. *Research and Advocacy Digest* 8(2).

——. ed. (2006). Sexual harassment. *Research and Advocacy Digest.* The Washington Coalition of Sexual Assault Papers.

ASCA (American School Counselor Association). (2004). *Ethical Standards for School Counselors,* Section A.2.b. Available at: www.schoolcounselor.org/files/ethical%20standards.pdf.

Beidler v. North Thurston County (Wash.) School District. (2000). No. 99-2-00236-6 (Thurston County Super. Ct. July 18, 2000) (unpublished).

Bethel School District v. Fraser. (1986). 478 U.S. 675.

Beussink v. Woodland School District. (1998). 30 F. Supp. 2d 1175 (E.D. Mo. 1998).

Board of Education of Westside Community Schools v. Mergens. (1990). 496 U.S. 226.

Davis v. Monroe County Bd. of Education. (1999). 526 U.S. 629, 119 S. Ct. 1661.

DeSouza, E. R., & Ribeiro, J. (2005). Bullying and sexual harassment among Brazilian high school students. *Journal of Interpersonal Violence* 20(9): 1018–38.

Doe v. Pulaski County Special School District. (2001). 263 F.3d 833 (8th Cir. 2001).

Dragen, E. F. (2006). Sexual harassment: Recent case law. Paper presented at Education Law Association Conference, Nassau, The Bahamas, November.

Emmett v. Kirkland School District No. 415. (2000). 92 F.Supp. 2d 1088.

Fineran, S., & Bennett, L. (2000). Gender and power issues of peer sexual harassment among teenagers. *Journal of Interpersonal Violence* 14(6): 626–41.

Franklin v. Gwinnett County Public Schools. (1992). 502 U.S. 60.

Gebser v. Lago Vista Independent School Dist. (1998). 524 U.S. 274.

GLSEN (Gay, Lesbian and Straight Education Network). (2001). National School Climate Survey. Available at: www.glsen.org/tmplates/news/record .html?section=20&record (retrieved July 24, 2007).

Goldstein, N. (2001). *Zero indifference: A how-to guide for ending name-calling in schools.* New York: Gay Lesbian and Straight Education Network.

Hawkins v. Sarasota County School Board. (2003). 322 F.3d 1279 (11th Cir. 2003).

Hazelwood School District v. Kuhlmeier. (1988). 484 U.S. 260.

Jane Doe v. Dallas Independent School District. (2001). WL 1593694 (N.D. Tex. Jul. 16, 2002).

J.S. v. Bethlehem Area School District. (2002). 807 A.2d 847 (Pa. 2002).

Koepels, S., & Dupper, D. R. (1999). School-based peer sexual harassment. *Child Welfare* 78: 435–60.

Lovell v. Poway Unified School District. (1994). 847 F. Supp. 780, 783 (S.D. Cal. 1994).

McGrath, M. J. (2007). *School bullying.* Thousand Oaks, CA: Corwin Press.

Meritor Savings Bank v. Vinson. (1986). 477 U.S. 57.

Merriam-Webster. (2004). *Merriam-Webster's Collegiate Dictionary,* 11th edition. Springfield, MA: Merriam-Webster.

Murdock, K. W., & Kysilko, D. (1998). *Sexual harassment in schools: What it is, what to do.* Alexandria, VA: National Association of State Boards of Education.

Murrell v. School Dist. No. 1. (1999). 186 F.3d 1238 (10th Cir. 1999).

Nabozny v. Podlesny. (1996). 92 F.3d 446 (7th cir. 1996).

National School Boards Association. (1996). *Sexual harassment: What it is and why should I care? A video based training program and prevention guide.* Alexandria, VA: National Association of State Boards of Education.

NOW Legal Defense and Education Fund. (1999). *Sexual harassment in the schools.* Available at: www.legalmomentum.org/issues/edu/blueprint.pdf (retrieved May 23, 2007).

OCR (Office for Civil Rights). (n.d.a.). Questions and answers regarding Title IX Procedural Requirements. Available at: www.usdoj.gov/crt/cor/coord/Title IXQandA.htm (retrieved January 29, 2007).

———. (n.d.b.) Sexual harassment: It's not academic. Available at: www.ed.gov/print/about/offices/list/ocr/docs/ocrshpam.html (retrieved May 29, 2007).

———. (1997). *Sexual harassment guidance: Harassment of students by school employees, other students or third parties.* Available at: www.ed.gov/about/offices/ list/ocr/docs/sexhar01.html.

———. (1999). *Protecting students from harassment and hate crimes: A guide for schools.* Available at: www.ed.gov/offices/OCR/archives/Harassment/index .html (retrieved June, 2007).

———. (2001). *Revised sexual harassment guidance: Harassment of students by school employees, other students or third parties.* Washington, DC: U.S. Department of Education.

O'Shaughnessy, M., Russell, S., Heck, K., Calhoun, C., & Laub, C. (2004). *Safe Place to Learn: Consequences of harassment based on actual or perceived sexual orientation and gender non-conformity and steps for making schools safe.* Davis: California Safe Schools Coalition and 4-H Center for Youth Development, University of California–Davis.

OSSTF. (Ontario Secondary School Teachers' Federation) (OSSTF). (1994). *Student to student sexual harassment: Final report on Phase 1.* Toronto, ON: OSSTF.

Permanent Commission on the Status of Women. (1995). *In our backyard: Sexual harassment in Connecticut's public high schools.* Hartford, CT: Author.

Ray v. Antioch Sch. Dist. (2000). 107 F. Supp. 2d 1165 (N.D. Cal. 2000).

Remafedi, R. J., & Deisher, R. (1991). Risk factors for attempted suicide in gay and bisexual youth. *Pediatrics* 87(6): 869–75.

Rhode Island Task Force on Gay and Lesbian Youth. (1996). School shouldn't hurt: Lifting the burden from gay, lesbian, bisexual and transgendered youth. Available from: http://members.tripod.com/~twood/safeschools .html (retrieved September, 5, 2007).

Rowe, L. L. (1996). The role of school counselors in confronting peer sexual harassment. *School Counselor* 43(3): 196–207.

Schoop, R. J., & Edwards, D. L. (1994). *Sexual harassment in our schools: What parents and teachers need to know to spot it and stop it.* Boston: Allyn and Bacon.

Schwarz, W. (2000). *Preventing student sexual harassment.* ERIC Digest Number 160. ERIC Educational Reports, December. Available at: www.eric.ed.gov/ ERICWebPortal/Home.portal (retrieved January 22, 2007).

Sousa, C., Bancroft, L., & German, T. (1986). *Preventing Teen Dating Violence— Three session curriculum for teaching adolescents.* Cambridge, MA: Dating Violence Intervention Project.

Stein, N. (1995). Sexual harassment in school: The public performance of gendered violence. Harvard Educational Review, 65. 145–162.

Stein, N., Marshall, N., & Tropp, L. (1993). Secrets in public: Sexual harassment in our schools. A joint project of the NOW Legal Defense and Education Fund and Wellesley College Center for Research on Women. Wellesley, MA: Center for Research on Women, Wellesley College.

Stone, C. B. (2000). Advocacy for sexual harassment victims: Legal support and ethical aspects. *Professional School Counseling.* 4.

Stone, M. and Couch, S. (2004). Peer sexual harassment among high school students: Teachers' attitudes, perceptions, and responses. *High School Journal* 88:1 1–13.

Strauss, S., & Espeland, P. (1992). *Sexual harassment and teens: A program for positive change*. Santa Cruz, CA: ETR Associates.

Tinker v. Des Moines Independent Community School District. (1969). 393 U.S. 503.

United States Equal Employment Opportunity Commission. (1997). *Enforcement Guidances and Related Documents*. www.eeoc.gov (retrieved July 12, 2007).

Willard, N. (2005). *Responding to the challenge of On-line social aggression, threats, and distress*. USA: Research Press.

Vance v. Spencer County Public School District. (2000). 231 F. 3d 253 (6th Cir. 2000).

Witkowska, E. (2005). Sexual harassment in schools: The concept and its perceptions. Stockholm, Sweden: Arbetslivsinstitutet. Available at: www.skoliv.nu/forskningsprojekt/trakasserer.pdf (retrieved June 20, 2007).

Yaffee, E. (1995). Expensive, illegal and wrong: Sexual harassment in our schools. *Phi Delta Kappan* 77(3): 1–18.

About the Author

Jan Cantrell has taught education law and other education subjects to graduate and undergraduate students in higher education for seventeen years in Oklahoma and Idaho. Prior to that she taught English in secondary schools in Colorado and Oklahoma for twenty years. Her Ph.D., from the University of Oklahoma, is in educational administration with an emphasis on education law. Her two professional passions are teaching school law classes and teaching teachers and future teachers how to teach, not just present. She is determined to help teachers and administrators make school a safe place where students want to come. Her awards include Teacher of the Year, Best Community Teacher, and Favorite Teacher numerous times.